DEV

Praise be to
God, who has
not rejected my
prayer.

—Psalm 66:20

DECEMBER

Photo © istock

Gary Allen, Editor

Pondering God's Purpose

After this his wife Elizabeth became pregnant and for five months remained in seclusion (Luke 1:24).

Scripture: **Luke 1:24, 25**
Song: **"Alone with God"**

I needed a break—or at least a short sabbatical. Maybe our church building project had affected me more than I realized. Although I enjoyed being a minister, my heart was somewhere else these days. My interests were changing. After decades of ministry, did God have other plans for me? Why would God ask me to start writing now?

I needed time to mull things over. I remembered that the apostle Paul sought solitude after his conversion experience on the Damascus Road. He allowed time for God's message to saturate his heart (see Galatians 1:16-18). Moses spent time on Mount Sinai. Elijah rested by a brook. Jesus himself sought out the quietness of the wilderness. In seclusion, they all communed with the Father. Similarly, Elizabeth remained by herself to reflect on the favor of God.

We today also need time alone with God. Thankfully, He draws us to "isolated places" in our lives that we might simply wait on Him. In the quiet, we can ponder His goodness and learn more of His purposes.

Draw me away, **O Lord,** *to that secret place of prayer. Help me listen closely for Your still, small voice. In Christ Jesus, I pray. Amen.*

December 1, 2. **Charles E. Harrel** has been a minister for more than 30 years. He currently directs His Place Outreach in Portland, Oregon.

Just Tell It

Come and listen, all you who fear God; let me tell you what he has done for me (Psalm 66:16).

Scripture: **Psalm 66:16-20**
Song: **"I Love to Tell the Story"**

The gold-plated fish hook on the man's shirt collar grabbed my attention. It reminded me of my dad; he often pinned his favorite fishing fly or lure on his hat. After I'd snuck several glances, the man walked over and introduced himself. Our conversation soon turned to fishing.

I discovered this gold hook was John's favorite one; he had caught more fish with it than any other. He told me that he once hooked a 200-pounder with it!

John always kept his favorite hook handy in case he saw a fish. In fact, he said, he had one on the line now (and he started to tug on his collar as if a fish were nibbling). That's when I realized John had been fishing for me. With his hook set, John told me the story of his own experience of being caught—by the greatest fisherman of all.

Our witness matters. People may dismiss our doctrine, or disagree with our beliefs, but they cannot deny what God has done in our lives. If we'll just tell them how God has graciously reached into our hearts, we can let Him take care of the rest.

Father, I know we all have different stories. Some have experienced Your healing, others a wonderful answer to prayer. But all of us have known Your unconditional favor through Christ's work of atonement. Help me to tell of Your great goodness in my life. In Jesus' name, amen.

Trusting for Each Step

Blessed is the man who makes the LORD his trust, who does not look to the proud, to those who turn aside to false gods (Psalm 40:4).

Scripture: **Psalm 40:1-5**
Song: **"I Could Not Do Without Thee"**

As I read Psalm 40 for my morning devotions, the fourth verse really seemed to stand out. I realized how often I am tempted to trust in people or things more than the Lord. Why? For one thing, we're constantly bombarded by media messages calling us to find our security elsewhere—with all kinds of appealing false gods.

And those gods come in many forms, don't they? Yet science and technology can't solve all of our problems. And mere possessions won't deliver a solid and settled joy. Even modern medicine—a great boon to civilization—can subtly pull us away from ultimate trust in God for our well-being. As educator Harold W. Dodds once said: "The way to be safe is never to be secure. . . . Each one of us requires the spur of insecurity to force us to do our best." Perhaps that is why God calls us to walk by faith and not by sight, one step at a time.

Dear Lord, I live in a world filled with so much that is questionable—or downright evil. Help me resist the allure of finite pleasures and trust You, instead, for every good thing. In the holy name of Jesus, my Lord and Savior, I pray. Amen.

December 3–9. **Gerry Kershner** writes from his home in Lancaster County, Pennsylvania. In addition to devotionals, he writes poetry and magazine articles.

Troubled by Good News?

Mary was greatly troubled at his words and wondered what kind of greeting this might be (Luke 1:29).

Scripture: **Luke 1:26-29**
Song: **"Joy to the World"**

Mary later exhibited tremendous joy and faith concerning this miraculous event. But why was she initially so troubled at Gabriel's words, wondering "what kind of greeting this might be"? This sudden introduction was a great surprise, of course—even a bit shocking. And no doubt Mary needed time to adjust to her new role.

We too may initially react to good news with a troubled spirit. In a wonderful 1983 film about redemption, *Tender Mercies*, the main character (played by Robert Duvall) is baptized and changed forever. But he later says to the lady who brought him into the church: "I prayed last night to know: *Why?* . . . I don't know why I wandered to this part of Texas, and you took me in, pitied me, and helped me to straighten out. . . . Why did that happen? You see, I don't trust happiness. I never did and never will."

We may not be able to explain (or fully trust) the sudden goodness of God in our lives, for sometimes that grace enters in almost shocking ways. We are right to be troubled—at least for awhile—until our consternation turns to unspeakable joy.

Dear Father, during this season when we celebrate the birth of Your Son, I am overwhelmed with Your sudden entrance into this world. Help me to accept Your many good gifts with joy. In Jesus' name, amen.

Let the Kingdom Show Through!

He will reign over the house of Jacob forever; his kingdom will never end (Luke 1:33).

Scripture: **Luke 1:30-33**
Song: **"There's a Song in the Air"**

Like many other Christians, I'm distressed by the crass commercialism and secular activities associated with Christmas in our culture. Every year we seem to experience less of the true meaning of Christ's incarnation.

As I read Luke 1:33 I wonder what the angel Gabriel means when he says that Jesus' kingdom will never end. Then I'm reminded that (at least for now) Jesus' realm is not a political, earthly kingdom. He refused political rule during His time on earth. No, Jesus reigns forever in the hearts of His followers, a kingdom that will never end.

As followers of Jesus we can share His love, His joy, and His peace with others during the Christmas season and throughout the year. We can do this no matter how others celebrate. In this way we can be a part of maintaining Jesus' kingdom and even helping spread it in our neighborhoods and throughout the world. As Jesus himself said, "The kingdom of God is within you" (Luke 17:21). But will we let His reign in our hearts be visible in the most practical and loving forms of outreach?

Lord, help me to keep my eyes, mind, and heart on You, continually reminding me that Your Kingdom is within me. And do move me to share Your love, Your joy, and Your peace with others during this Christmas season. In the name of Jesus, who came as Lord and Savior of all, I pray. Amen.

Back to Basics

The holy one to be born will be called the Son of God (Luke 1:35).

Scripture: **Luke 1:34, 35**
Song: **"Silent Night"**

For many of us, the Christmas season is harried and hurried. We have gifts to make or buy, boxes to wrap, cards to address and send, parties to plan, food to buy and prepare, and church activities to fit into our busy schedules. Most of these activities are good, but I'm thinking of "going back to the basics."

I'm starting with the basic question, "What is Christmas all about?" In today's verse the angel tells Mary that the child to be born will be called the Son of God. In that brief announcement we can see that Christmas is really the most important event in the history of the world. God came to the world as a flesh-and-blood human being!

In light of this amazing truth, all of our Christmas activities take on new meaning. The gifts, cards, food, parties, and church activities now all become our part of celebrating the radical entrance of the Son of God. What a birthday this is—calling us to slow down, to contemplate its miraculous unfolding, to make room for many silent nights of praise.

Dear Father in Heaven, *I come to You during this harried and hurried season, asking You to help me get back to the basics. Keep me focused on the great miracle of Your Son coming in person to love Your world. And help me love Him with all my heart in return. In His name, I pray. Amen.*

Mary, the Lord's Servant

"I am the Lord's servant," Mary answered. "May it be to me as you have said" (Luke 1:38).

Scripture: **Luke 1:36-38**
Song: **"Mary, Did You Know?"**

Rereading the wonderful story of Christmas in the first chapter of Luke's gospel, I am struck by Mary's humble acceptance of the angel's dramatic announcement that she is to be pregnant. And her child was to be called the Son of the Most High!

After all this fanfare, she simply answers, "I am the Lord's servant. May it be to me as you have said" (1:38). Yes, she may have been a bit confused, or troubled, but she apparently did not need to know all of the minor details and long-term implications, as I usually do. God said it, and that was enough. Such child-like faith is a lesson I often need to relearn.

I think any of us can learn much from Mary. We don't normally receive angelic visitations, but we do often experience God moving in ways we do not understand. And this is where we can remember Mary's example. Rather than trying to understand the big picture all at once, we can simply take the next step with God.

Dear Lord and Master, *thank You so much for Mary and the many other biblical role models You've given me, that I may lead a life pleasing to You. I too am Your servant. So help me live with simple, child-like faith in Your good will and guidance in my life. In the name of the Father, the Son, and the Holy Spirit, I pray. Amen.*

Elizabeth's Joy and Faith

As soon as the sound of your greeting reached my ears, the baby in my womb leaped for joy (Luke 1:44).

Scripture: **Luke 1:39-45**
Song: **"My Faith Looks Up to Thee"**

We can hardly imagine the joy that Elizabeth felt when Mary visited her. She who had been childless during her normal child-bearing years was now pregnant. She must have been overjoyed when she immediately recognized that her relative, Mary, was also pregnant in a miraculous way. Elizabeth's joy in the autumn of her life must have been especially sweet.

Yet through all those childless years, Elizabeth kept her strong faith in God. She was upright in the sight of God. She observed all of the commandments and regulations blamelessly. Later, she believed that the One who made the promise would keep the promise. Simply put, she kept the faith.

Many of us have dreams that remain unfulfilled, causing us, at times, to doubt God's goodwill toward us. Yet, like Elizabeth, we need to keep the faith, because our faith is more important than our dreams. As writer Henry Thoreau once said: "The smallest seed of faith is better than the largest fruit of happiness."

Dear Lord, strengthen my faith. Help me to remain true and faithful even when I have no visible evidence, like Elizabeth during her childless years. Help me to keep the faith so I may also experience joy as Elizabeth did. In Jesus' name I pray. Amen.

Mary's Song of Praise

My soul glorifies the Lord and my spirit rejoices in God my Savior (Luke 1:46, 47).

Scripture: **Luke 1:46-56**
Song: **"How Majestic Is Your Name"**

I am humbled by Mary's song of praise in these ten verses, traditionally called the *Magnificat*. After a spontaneous outburst of praise for her personal blessing, she continues to praise God for His mercy, power, and goodness in the past as well as the present.

I must confess that far too often I do not praise God and give Him the glory for the small, and sometimes even the larger, blessings in my life. Oh yes, I pray on a daily basis like many other Christians. But my prayer requests often far outnumber my praise items. Obviously, Mary had many personal prayer needs at this time, but none of them are included in this short song of praise.

Study of this song has convinced me to make a deliberate, personal effort to include more and more praise in my prayer life. In fact, I hope it will become a spontaneous and constant part of my relationship with God. After all, prayer is primarily an opening of hearts up to God, just as Mary did. Sometimes it is simply a wordless adoration or a period of silent listening for Him. But couldn't many of us use a little boost to our prayer lives by adding small songs of praise to our daily devotional times?

Dear Lord, *You are so good! Help me to praise you spontaneously and sincerely this day. In Your holy name I pray. Amen.*

Messengers

See, I will send my messenger, who will prepare the way before me (Malachi 3:1).

Scripture: **Malachi 3:1-4**
Song: **"If Jesus Goes With Me"**

When I feel unimportant, I recall the words I once heard a minister preach: "You may be the only Bible some people will ever read." John the Baptist must have understood this thoroughly. He was the messenger God chose to prepare the way for Jesus' arrival.

On the face of it, John was unimpressive. He lived in the wilderness, ate bugs, and wore strange clothes. Yet people flocked to hear the message of repentance he preached. They came, not because John was attractive, but because he was a faithful messenger, telling the people what God wanted them to know.

We may never know the impact we have on the people we encounter, day in and day out. A kindness done to a stranger, a hug given a stressed-out coworker, or time spent with a little child may seem like simple, unnoticeable acts. But to God, they are a witness to the world of Christ's love. When we allow God to use us as messengers of the gospel, we may even amaze ourselves.

Lord, I feel so unworthy of the calling to be a messenger of Your good news. Help me be faithful, in word and deed—and be on the lookout for those in any kind of need. In the name of Christ I pray. Amen.

December 10–16. **Lisa Konzen** works for United Way in Janesville, Wisconsin. She also writes health articles for seniors in her local newspaper, *The Janesville Gazette*.

Standing Up

But his mother spoke up and said, "No! He is to be called John" (Luke 1:60).

Scripture: **Luke 1:57-61**
Song: **"Stand Up, Stand Up for Jesus"**

I used to be quite a pushover. If my food was served cold at a restaurant, I'd meekly eat it instead of sending it back. If I wasn't satisfied with something I bought, I'd stash it away in my closet instead of returning it to the store for a refund.

But not anymore. What made the difference? The day I realized that some things are worth standing up for. My father was in the hospital, and because he had many health problems, full and complete information about his status wasn't always communicated very well. I had to approach doctors and nurses rather assertively for the answers I needed.

It taught me a valuable lesson: Sometimes, you just have to be tough. Not unkind, and certainly not violent. But tough. It all depends on what you're standing up for. I imagine Elizabeth trembled a little when her relatives challenged her decision to name her son John. But she knew that was what God wanted her to do. So, despite being a woman in a society that did not highly value a woman's opinion, Elizabeth stood up for God.

Holy God, too often I've been timid when I should have been bold. Yet You are the source of all my courage. Fill me with Your presence to the extent that I have no room left for fear. In the name of Jesus, amen.

Tongue Un-Tied

Immediately his mouth was opened and his tongue was loosed, and he began to speak, praising God (Luke 1:64).

Scripture: Luke 1:62-66
Song: "Praise the Savior"

Have you ever been tongue-tied when trying to talk about your faith? You know you should say something, but it's so difficult. Maybe you're going through a rough time, and bearing witness for God seems to require more faith than you feel you have.

Zechariah knew about being tongue-tied. When the angel Gabriel told him his elderly, barren wife Elizabeth would bear a son, he asked for proof. His lack of trust was met with a stern promise from Gabriel that Zechariah would not be able to speak until the child was born. And sure enough, Zechariah was mute until the day he said, "His name is John" (1:63).

I think we can learn a lesson from Zechariah. His lack of trust in God led him to mute ineffectiveness. Similarly, when our faith falters, we may find it difficult to speak about the good news of the gospel. But the same Holy Spirit who loosened Zechariah's tongue and restored his faith can do the same for us. Our simple willingness to be used by Him is the first movement toward a full-bodied trust that won't falter.

Word of God, speak through me. My tongue is dry, and my heart is empty without You. But when You dwell in me, rivers of blessings pour forth from my lips as I sing Your praises! In the name of Jesus, amen.

Without Fear

He has raised up a horn of salvation . . . to rescue us from the hand of our enemies, and to enable us to serve him without fear (Luke 1:69, 74).

Scripture: **Luke 1:67-75**
Song: **"All Your Anxiety"**

You've probably heard of the fight-or-flight response. It's the wonderful system God designed in our bodies that helps us react to dangerous situations. When we're in crisis, the hormone adrenaline is released. For example, a grizzly bear challenges us in the woods. We can either try to tackle him to the ground or . . . run away. Fast!

We rarely face grizzlies in modern living today. Yet, our bodies react the same way when we feel under pressure day after day, or experience even a minor conflict with a coworker or spouse. Adrenaline still shoots into our hearts; we react with fear—and fight or flee.

Problem is, when the crisis passes, many of us can't seem to turn off the response! Chronic fear can contribute to the development of generalized anxiety, depression, and a host of physical maladies, including heart disease. Our hectic lives have turned what was once a blessing from God into a curse.

But it doesn't have to be that way. In Christ, we are set free. We'll still face stress, but as we cast our cares upon our Savior, we can let go and let God rescue us.

Dear God, *it's so easy to become afraid these days. But You asked me to cast my cares upon You, so that's what I'm going to do. Through Christ, amen.*

Knowing the Word

To give his people the knowledge of salvation through the forgiveness of their sins (Luke 1:77).

Scripture: **Luke 1:76-80**
Song: **"More About Jesus"**

The minister of my church is a strong believer in Bible study, and with good reason. Because he is so faithful in teaching the truth of God's Word, we know the history and mystery of our faith. History, because he painstakingly presents the narrative of the Scripture, exploring the time lines and themes.

But he goes way beyond that, teaching us the mystery of the grace of our Savior, Jesus Christ, and the way His life, death, and resurrection free us to serve Him joyfully.

And serve Him we do. From hunger walks to "Christmas in July" fund raisers for the local food pantry, our church practices what our minister preaches. New ministries inside and outside of the church are continually springing up. But if all this sounds like bragging, that's because it is. Not about our members, or even about our minister. We're just responding to the gift of salvation freely given that we learn about as we study Scripture. All the praise, glory, and honor go to Jesus, the Word of Life who writes His gospel across the lives of His people. For without Him, we can do nothing.

O Lord, help me to rededicate myself to studying the Scripture each day. I want to be knowledgeable so I can share the treasures of Your truth with every open-hearted person I meet. In Jesus' name, amen.

Pedigree or Mutt?

Do not begin to say to yourselves, "We have Abraham as our father." For I tell you that out of these stones God can raise up children for Abraham (Luke 3:8).

Scripture: **Luke 3:7-14**
Song: **"A Child of the King"**

All my life we've had dogs. I remember Bagel, so named because we were told she was a beagle, only to learn later that she was a Pit Bull mix. Peggy, a black Labrador retriever, who was so smart and loving. And Princess Su Linn, a Lhasa Apso who was the only pure-bred dog our family ever had.

Pedigreed or mutt, it really doesn't matter. What matters with dogs is not who their parents were, but the love given by their owners. A dog won't snub us because his sire was a best in show. Dogs stand on their own four paws, protecting and loving us because they're part of our family.

We can learn a lot from our pooch pals. It doesn't matter what our name is, where we're from, or how much money sits in our bank account. What matters in the church is that we're all part of God's family. It has nothing to do with any effort on our part. God adopted us and calls us to love each other as brothers and sisters in Christ.

Heavenly Father, *thank You for adopting me into Your family as a precious child. Help me to remember the pure grace that made it possible—and therefore to love unconditionally all my siblings in the faith. I pray this prayer in the name of Jesus, my merciful Savior and Lord. Amen.*

Proud to Be Humble

John answered them all, "I baptize you with water. But one more powerful than I will come, the thongs of whose sandals I am not worthy to untie" (Luke 3:16).

Scripture: **Luke 3:15-20**
Song: **"The Unveiled Christ"**

Have you ever heard someone complain about having to play second fiddle? Perhaps it was an employee whose co-worker was just promoted. "I hate playing second fiddle to him," the disgruntled worker might grumble. Playing second fiddle means you are not the one in charge, not the one getting all the attention.

But have you ever wondered what the phrase literally means? An orchestra has sections and subsections. Within the strings are violins, in subsets of first and second violins (violins being the dressed-up name for fiddles). The role of the second violins is to support the work of the first violins, enhancing them with glorious harmony.

John the Baptist wasn't ashamed to play second fiddle to Jesus. He knew he had a job to do, and he wasn't in it for the limelight. For him, playing second fiddle was right because he knew Jesus was the Savior whose sacrifice would save him and the world. Perhaps next time we're asked to serve in the shadows, we'll remember the prophet in the wilderness who was proud to be humble.

Dear God and Father, *may my thoughts, words, and actions take the spotlight off me and glorify You. Let me bring harmony to Your kingdom. Through Your precious Son, Jesus Christ, I pray. Amen.*

Making It a List

Sing to the LORD a new song. . . . Splendor and majesty are before him; strength and glory are in his sanctuary (Psalm 96:1, 6).

Scripture: **Psalm 96:1-6**
Song: **"Glorious Is Thy Name"**

I'm a year-round list-maker. Lists keep me focused—especially at Christmas time. Let's see, what do I need to do in order to be ready? Cards, decorations, gifts, parties, programs . . . and on it goes.

I do something similar when I study God's Word. If I come to a passage that includes a list of God's attributes or commands, I love to list them in my journal. Then I might use a Bible dictionary to jot some definitions next to each item. Even the subtle differences I find between quite similar words give me much food for thought. The next step is to consider how to apply what I've learned.

A particular favorite this time of year is the list of names in Isaiah 9:6: Wonderful Counselor, Mighty God, Everlasting Father, Prince of Peace. Even today's passage lends itself to such a word study with phrases like: praise His name, proclaim His salvation, declare His glory, splendor and majesty, strength and glory. What do each of these mean to you?

Lord, Your Word is so rich. May I pause at even familiar words and find in them a new song to sing Your praise. Through Christ my Lord, amen.

December 17–23. **Susan Miholer,** a grandmother and special education assistant, owns Picky, Picky Ink, her editorial service in Salem, Oregon.

The Trinity of the Slide

Give him the name Jesus, because he will save his people from their sins (Matthew 1:21).

Scripture: **Matthew 1:18b-21**
Song: **"The Name of Jesus"**

"Grandma, come get me!" Four-year-old Nicholas was at the top of the slide at a fast-food restaurant, too scared to come down. I assumed some uncomfortable positions as I crawled through the not-quite-adult-sized tunnels to get to him, and then I rode down the slide with him. Not my most dignified grandmotherly moment! He, on the other hand, thought it was great fun. I kept envisioning the newspaper headline: "Grandmother Stuck—Fire Department Summoned."

I didn't feel very god-like that day; in fact, I was glad there were few witnesses to my actions and attitude. But later I saw the whole episode as a picture of what God did for us. As the Father, He saw our need of a Savior. As the Son, He assumed the uncomfortable positions of the Incarnation to rescue me. And as the Holy Spirit, He rides with me through the twists and turns of this slide-ride we call life.

Jesus. There's just something about that name—something that tells us so much about God that we can never comprehend it all.

Heavenly Father, *when I consider how You reached down through Your Son, I'm humbled that You included me in Your great plan of salvation. Thank You for the sacrifice of the Incarnation! In Jesus' name, amen.*

A New Chapter

So Joseph also went . . . to Bethlehem. . . . He went there to register with Mary (Luke 2:4, 5).

Scripture: **Luke 2:1-5**
Song: **"O Little Town of Bethlehem"**

During the last few weeks of my pregnancies, waddling anywhere was a challenge. Travel for any reason other than essential errands and appointments was pretty much out of the question.

Mary probably wasn't eager to travel from Nazareth to Bethlehem in her condition. But regardless of the discomforts involved, she was no doubt relieved to be getting away from the whispers and judgmental stares in her old neighborhood. She was probably both exhilarated and frightened about her new role as mother too—a new chapter in her life. Bethlehem might well provide a clean slate for her and Joseph.

When God ushers in a new chapter in our lives, we often experience the same emotional mix—the exhilaration, yet the questions about what is happening and why things are unfolding the way they are. And, like Mary, we can face the challenge with a similar response: "May it be to me as you have said" (Luke 1:38).

Facing a life-change in this season of your life? Look to God as He leads you into a new chapter.

*Thank You, **God,** that You have gone before me into the unknown of my life. Allow me to trust You for the grace, strength, and wisdom to face today's challenges. In the name of Jesus, my Savior, I pray. Amen.*

No Room in the Family?

There was no room for them in the inn (Luke 2:7).

Scripture: **Luke 2:6, 7**
Song: **"No Room in the Inn"**

At the birth of my first grandchild, we grandparents practically elbowed each other out of the way to be first in the room to see our new baby boy. But Scripture is strangely silent about Mary and Joseph's families. I would think that several members of Joseph's family would have been in Bethlehem. Didn't they have to go there to register as well? If this was Joseph's ancestral home, I'd expect there may have been relatives in Bethlehem with whom they could have stayed. But they seemed so alone in that place.

I know Scripture doesn't give us all the details, but I'm wondering if Mary's circumstances had ostracized Joseph and Mary so much that even close family members wouldn't extend hospitality to them—or at least some loving concern. That would take the phrase "no room for them in the inn" (2:7) to another level, wouldn't it? Not only was there no room in the inn, there may have been no room in the family circle.

Yet Jesus' earthly parents model for me the response I should have when I feel cut off from others. Follow God anyway.

Father, I sometimes feel there's no room for me in certain situations because I've chosen to follow You along the narrow way. At those times, may I rest assured that You are always with me. Through Christ, amen.

Creative Announcement

Today in the town of David a Savior has been born to you; he is Christ the Lord (Luke 2:11).

Scripture: **Luke 2:8-14**
Song: **"Angels We Have Heard on High"**

People have gotten creative with birth announcements lately, as the computer provides all kinds of new ways to announce a baby's entrance into the world. Families design entire websites to share the news. I've even seen custom-printed wrappers that slip over a regular chocolate bar. The front of the label (and its color) let people know the baby's vital statistics. And the parents' names replace the standard ingredients label.

But the most creative of all birth announcements occurred on a hillside over 2,000 years ago as a bunch of ordinary (and probably scruffy) shepherds settled their sheep and themselves for the night. As they adjusted their cloaks to ward off the evening chill, and breathed that last relaxed sigh of impending sleep, an angel amid the glory of the Lord delivered awesome good news. And then the sky seemed to explode as the heavenly host underscored the grand message.

No other birth in history has been announced in such magnificent style. Nor has any other birth in history had the same eternal consequences. No wonder the angels praised God!

Eternal God, *may I, like the angels, praise You and say, Glory to God in the highest! In the name of the incarnate Christ I pray. Amen.*

Different Reactions

Mary treasured up all these things and pondered them in her heart (Luke 2:19).

Scripture: **Luke 2:15-20**
Song: **"O Come, Let Us Adore Him"**

Different people react differently to good news. Some clap, some cry, some dance, and some just stand there looking surprised. I've done all four—and sometimes two or three at the same time.

Recovering from the spectacle of God's glory and the good news of Christ's birth, the shepherds couldn't get to Bethlehem fast enough. Having seen the baby, their exuberance bubbled over as they told everyone of the angel's announcement and what they had seen. People were astonished. Even without e-mail, the news traveled quickly. But Mary, precious Mary, the one who had known for months whose child this was, quietly pondered what was happening, filing away memories of her Son.

Emotions run high at Christmas time. Like the shepherds, we may push and shove to get there first. We may be so excited about the good news of Christmas that we sing the familiar carols with new enthusiasm, astonished by the discovery of new facets in the familiar story. But like Mary, I also want to carve out times of quiet reflection upon who Jesus really is—my Lord and my God.

Dear Father, the birth of Your Son changed the course of history. May I understand a piece of the Christmas story in a new way this year. Keep my focus on who Christ is and why He came. In His name I pray. Amen.

Who's the Author?

Ascribe to the Lord the glory due his name; bring an offering and come into his courts (Psalm 96:8).

Scripture: **Psalm 96:7-13**
Song: **"Creation's Lord, We Give Thee Thanks"**

We don't use the word "ascribe" very often anymore. The dictionary says it suggests an "inferring or conjecturing of cause, quality, or authorship." If you're a Shakespeare scholar or an expert on Picasso, you know what to look for in a specific play or work of art to indicate its creator. Sometimes, though, even the experts don't agree as to whom a particular work ought to be ascribed.

But there is no disagreement in today's passage about who is responsible for, who is the author of, all the beauty in nature. Every aspect of the natural world—the seas, the hills, the forests, even the living beings—point us toward their creator. And that same author is the author of our salvation, the baby whose birth we celebrate at this time of year.

Born in obscurity, He is the author of this world and everything in it. And if anything good and admirable blossoms within our hearts . . . He is the author of all of those virtues too. For our heart is the place He has chosen to make His dwelling place. Ascribe glory to Him!

My Father in Heaven, Your Son came to the earth to be the author of my salvation. Thank You, from the bottom of my heart. I want to worship You in the same spontaneous way Your creation does, pointing others to You. In the name of the Father, the Son, and the Holy Spirit, I pray. Amen.

The First Christmas Gift-giver

That you may bring my salvation to the ends of the earth (Isaiah 49:6).

Scripture: **Isaiah 49:5, 6**
Song: **"It Came Upon the Midnight Clear"**

Our familiar white-bearded Santa harks back to a third-century bishop born in Turkey. Renowned for his humility and generosity, Nicholas became the patron saint of many nations, causes, and groups, including sailors and children. A body of legend grew around his person, including the idea that he dressed in red and gave gifts at Christmas time.

Poet Clement Moore leaned on such legends as he wrote the whimsical, "A Visit from St. Nicholas" in 1832 to amuse his children. But the reindeer-powered Christmas Eve trip around the world was Moore's unique idea. His poem gained immediate fame and imposed a curious persona on humble Nicholas that would have amazed him.

We need not fuss about the folklore from many lands that colors our Christmas celebrations. But tree lights, holly, and mistletoe must not overshadow the manger, where the true Gift-giver was born. He offers His gift to the ends of the earth, not once a year, but every day—and throughout all generations to every tribe and tongue.

Thank You, **Lord,** *for offering Your gift of eternal life to all, whether they have been naughty or nice. All praise to You, in Christ's name. Amen.*

December 24–30. **Lloyd Mattson** is a retired minister and author of Christian camping books. He and his wife, Elsie, live in Duluth, Minnesota.

Poor Joseph and Mary!

Joseph and Mary took him to Jerusalem to present him to the Lord . . . and to offer a sacrifice in keeping with what is said in the Law of the Lord" (Luke 2:22, 24).

Scripture: **Luke 2:21-24**
Song: **"Thou Didst Leave Thy Throne"**

Joseph and Mary came to the temple with birds, the sacrifice of the poor. Similarly, throughout His ministry, Jesus depended on others for food and shelter. Yet we seldom think of Jesus or His family as poor. After all, poverty is relative; our poorest seem rich beyond imagining to earth's millions who are starving.

While Jesus placed no premium on poverty, He spoke often about greed. That's why Christmas appeals move us to give to the needy, and we rightly feel good about doing so. The Magi, too, presented gifts, but we can't know the worth of those gifts until we know what they had left.

What do we have left? Our benevolent giving marks us as among earth's most generous people, yet America has little cause for pride. Consider what we keep! The American dream wears a dollar sign, and a good Christmas usually means retailers sold more than they did the year before.

The point is, giving isn't really giving until it costs us something. And at Christmas time we can remember: We celebrate the birth of a man who owned nothing.

Heavenly Father, *that I might embrace Your presence in me to the fullest, please help me loosen my grip on everything else. In Jesus' name, amen.*

A Devout Nobody

Now there was a man in Jerusalem, called Simeon, who was righteous and devout. He was waiting for the consolation of Israel, and the Holy Spirit was upon him (Luke 2:25).

Scripture: **Luke 2:25, 26**
Song: **"Spirit of Faith, Come Down"**

A remarkable man, Simeon. He held no office or honors, yet the Holy Spirit was upon him. How could that be? Pentecost was at least three years away. Was not that the day the Holy Spirit came?

We tend to arrange God's affairs according to our limited understandings, keeping Him safely within the boundaries of our doctrinal preferences. We ought not do that, for the sovereign God works where, when, and among whom He chooses, and that truth abides today.

Simeon came to the temple at just the right time. As far as he knew, it was an ordinary day. Many people, priests, Levites, scribes, and teachers of the law bustled about. Did any of them long for Messiah's coming? But Simeon had a God-ward heart, and the Holy Spirit had given him a remarkable promise.

That day Simeon's longing was fulfilled. And the least of Jesus' followers can draw comfort from Simeon, a devout nobody who longed to see the Christ.

Dear Father above, *grant me holy desires this day. And thank You for Your gift of the Holy Spirit, who fulfills the desires of my heart. I pray this prayer in the name of Jesus, my merciful Savior and Lord. Amen.*

Take Him to Your Heart

When the parents brought in the child Jesus to do for him what the custom of the Law required, Simeon took him in his arms and praised God (Luke 2:27, 28).

Scripture: **Luke 2:27, 28**
Song: **"Into My Heart"**

I once read a little anecdote about a shabby lad who rushed into a department store on Christmas Eve, just before the store's closing. Out of breath, he pled, "Could we borrow your Jesus? Ours got busted." That line was irresistible, and I later wrote a story about a clumsy young man who knocked over a Christmas tree and shattered the porcelain pieces of a nativity scene. The story's theme: We all need our own special relationship with Jesus

Simeon experienced this when Mary came to the temple bearing a precious, six-weeks-old bundle. The baby's humanity and deity wasn't the issue, nor was His transcendent holiness. Moving beyond theology, Simeon simply took the mystery of Incarnation into his arms. For those moments, he had his very own Jesus.

We can take Jesus to our heads and acknowledge His historic reality. That is well and good—and quite necessary. We can assign Him the highest place of transcendence in our doctrines and worship. But day by day, do we keep Him at the center of our lives? Simeon, a simple, devout man, took Jesus to heart—and praised God.

Father in Heaven, grant me each day a continuing sense of Your presence in my life, through the indwelling Christ. In His name I pray. Amen.

Marvelous Pronouncement

The child's father and mother marveled at what was said about him (Luke 2:33).

Scripture: **Luke 2:29-33**
Song: **"My Savior First of All"**

A quiet, elderly woman came to our small church. Though she had had no formal Bible training, she eventually became our favorite Sunday school teacher. One day my wife asked where she had gained such heart-warming, intriguing insights. The woman replied, "Elsie, it takes a lifetime to know the Scriptures." She might have added, "It takes a lifetime—and beyond—to know Jesus."

Joseph and Mary marveled at Simeon's song, and little wonder. They were ordinary folks; how could those things be?

Joseph had taken Mary to be his wife at great risk. Who would believe her story? She had endured birth pangs and held the newborn to her breast in a stable. She had not yet digested the angel Gabriel's mysterious words or the song of her cousin Elizabeth. Now could the new parents not marvel at Simeon's prophetic pronouncement?

We, too, will marvel as we grow in the grace and knowledge of our Lord. There is much, much more to Jesus than our quaint renditions of the Christmas story. It will take a lifetime and more to learn it all.

*Thank You, **Lord,** for the privilege of knowing You. As I open my heart to You daily in prayer, lead me into an ever deeper knowledge of Your presence and purpose in my life. In the name of my precious Savior, I pray. Amen.*

December 29

Couldn't Lie to Her

(And a sword will pierce through your own soul also), that thoughts out of many hearts may be revealed (Luke 2:35, *Revised Standard Version*).

Scripture: **Luke 2:34, 35**
Song: **"Grace and Truth Shall Mark the Way"**

I could not bring myself to lie to Mother. I lied easily to my sister, and I could stretch a point with my father, but I could not lie to Mother. A quiet, small woman, Mother seemed able to read my thoughts. I believed that because I knew her character. I could depend on her, and I couldn't imagine her telling a lie. I fully believed lying to her was useless; she would know the truth.

We were not an overtly religious household, and few Christian artifacts hung on our walls. We attended church faithfully, though, and rarely missed a mealtime prayer. The Bible was prominent, faith in Christ was genuine, and Mother was warm and affirming. She embodied what I imagined Jesus to be.

An early memory finds me snuggling close to Mother's breast in an heirloom rocking chair. As we rocked, "Jesus Loves Me" resonated from her. Mother loved me, she loved Jesus, and so did I, even at age three. Yes, even then I understood that nothing was hidden from Mother, nor from God.

Lord, we are all the products of what we've been taught by people we trust. Thank You for my own teachers. May I be trustworthy, so that those who follow me will be following You. Through Christ I pray. Amen.

A Touch from the Old

She was very old . . . . She never left the temple but worshiped night and day (Luke 2:36, 37).

Scripture: **Luke 2:36-38**
Song: **"Beyond the Sunset"**

August was old and dying. I was his young, green minister. He told me one day he had seen Jesus. It seems the Lord was standing in the meadow just beyond a small stream on his old country farm, beckoning. "I will go home soon," August said.

I smiled at the old man's odd vision and prepared to read a psalm. A thin, pale hand slipped over the page. "Read from your heart, my brother." That I couldn't do, and so he led me, verse by verse, through the beloved passage, his words tinged with the gentle accent of his homeland. Within a few days, August died.

Cherish your godly elders! They are wiser and closer to Heaven than younger people can be. Come to think of it, those who have eternal life can never grow old. They will change dwelling places, but they can never age. I think often of August. I'm glad Jesus came to him when he was very old, so he could touch the heart of a young, green minister.

*Thank You, **Lord,** for elderly friends. Throughout the new year, nudge me to spend more time with them, so they can minister to me in their special way. And help me to never look down on those who are close to seeing You, face to face. I pray this prayer in the name of Jesus my Savior. Amen.*

Praise from Deep Within

Praise the LORD from the earth, you great sea creatures and all ocean depths (Psalm 148:7).

Scripture: **Psalm 148:7-14**
Song: **"All Creatures of Our God and King"**

Beneath the ocean's depths exists an amazing world of God's creation that most of us will never see. Yet even nature unseen functions as a testimony to God and offers its praise to the one who sees it, created it, and maintains it. The depths of the earth's oceans, and the creatures contained within, cause us to marvel. So many small creatures, such as jellyfish, sand dollars, starfish, and sea horses. So many grand creatures, such as manatees, dolphins, sharks, and whales. So many shapes and sizes and colors of marine life grace the seas. Even in a fallen world, God's creation is breathtaking.

Like the creatures of the sea, we too praise the one who intricately designed and assembled us, He who maintains us and sustains us. We worship Him who knows us and loves us despite our sin.

The unseen in us? He sees our deepest hurts and cares. And like the rest of creation, we too praise God, especially when we live according to our ultimate purpose on earth: to become more and more like His Son, Jesus.

Sovereign God of all Creation, I worship You. And as I live each day on earth, may my life reflect Your greatness. In Jesus' name, amen.

December 31. **Brian J. Waldrop** is a freelance writer and professional copy editor. Originally from Champaign, Illinois, Brian now resides in Mt. Healthy, Ohio.

DEVOTIONS

*H*is name alone is exalted; his splendor is above the earth and the heavens.

—Psalm 148:13

JANUARY

Photo © Photodisc

Gary Allen, Editor

Celebrate!

Have the Israelites celebrate the Passover (Numbers 9:2).

Scripture: **Numbers 9:1-5**
Song: **"Celebrate Jesus"**

The Israelites were commanded to celebrate the Passover, their deliverance from Egypt. It's crazy, but sometimes—even most of the time—people need to be reminded to celebrate: to appreciate, to be thankful, to remember.

Celebrations are fun but often mean a lot of work. For example, the Passover feast required many preparations. Lambs had to be slaughtered, and other specific rituals precisely followed. Concerning the Passover, verse 3 says to "celebrate it at the appointed time, at twilight on the fourteenth day of this month, in accordance with all its rules and regulations." Most celebrations don't have to be so elaborate, but they still require a concerted effort to make them meaningful.

Surprisingly, celebration comes hard for many Christians. Rather than being party people, we're often seen as sober killjoys. Yet of all people, we have the best reasons to celebrate, for God has come into our world by His Son to bring us new life. And if we are going to celebrate that, then New Year's Day is a great time to start!

Lord, throughout the coming year, help me remember who You are and what You have done—and respond in celebration. In Jesus' name, amen.

January 1-6. **Brian J. Waldrop** is a freelance writer and professional copy editor. Originally from Champaign, Illinois, Brian now resides in Mt. Healthy, Ohio.

Passed Over

When I see the blood, I will pass over you (Exodus 12:13).

Scripture: **Exodus 12:11-14**
Song: **"There Is Power in the Blood"**

"Duck, duck, duck, duck, *goose!*" As a child playing Duck Duck Goose, I never liked being the goose. In that situation, I considered being "passed over" a good thing. The Jews celebrated a feast called Passover, commemorating their release from Egyptian bondage. Why that name? The Israelites' release occurred after the final plague, the death of Egypt's firstborn. The firstborn of the Israelites were spared because their families obeyed God and put lamb's blood on the door frames of their homes, a sign for the death angel to "pass over" them.

God's essential character of holiness and justice won't allow Him to merely pass over our sins as if nothing has happened. Christians are indeed forgiven, however, because of the blood of their Passover Lamb, Jesus Christ. Thus, like the Israelites escaping the tyranny of Egyptian slavery, we are freed from the eternal consequences of our sins. By His blood, we escape the impossible tyranny of attempting to earn God's acceptance by good works. As the writer to the Hebrews put it: "He entered the Most Holy Place once for all by his own blood, having obtained eternal redemption" (Hebrews 9:12).

God, I breathe a sigh of relief at being passed over, escaping the judgment for sin. Praise You for sending Jesus, my Passover lamb! May I always live gratefully and obediently, in light of His sacrifice. In His name, amen.

Got Some Growing Up to Do?

The child grew and became strong; he was filled with wisdom, and the grace of God was upon him (Luke 2:40).

Scripture: **Luke 2:39-45**
Song: **"The Guiding Hand"**

It was a simple, loving act springing from the innocent heart of a little girl. Without saying a word, she walked over to my father and unlocked the seat belt he was having trouble unfastening from a fun-park ride. It was a gesture of the heart, not done for a sticker or a prize.

A child's tender, trusting heart is often more gracious than our own. For example, young children usually aren't as skeptical as we adults are. When words come from a trusted source, such as a parent or a teacher, children believe what they are told. They haven't yet been scarred by the deceptions of the unscrupulous.

We, as adults, need to regain a simple trust in God and His Word. Jesus himself, in His human nature, had to grow in wisdom and maturity—and respond positively to the grace that came from the Father. We may be adults, but I suspect we each have such growing up to do. The key, for us, is to keep our hearts open to all that God desires to do within us and through us. It's the only way to grow strong in the spiritual life.

Dear God, help me recapture the wonder, purity, and innocence of a childlike trust in Your goodness and guidance. I long to be filled with Your wisdom and motivated by Your Kingdom plans. And by Your grace, let me act graciously toward others, as well. Thank You, in Jesus' name. Amen.

An Amazing God

Everyone who heard him was amazed (Luke 2:47).

Scripture: **Luke 2:46-50**
Song: **"I Stand Amazed in the Presence"**

Even as a mere boy, Jesus wowed people by what He said and did. These same reactions would follow Jesus throughout His adult life: "The people were amazed at his teaching" (Mark 1:22). "The disciples were amazed at his words" (Mark 10:24). "The men were amazed and asked, 'What kind of man is this?'" (Matthew 8:27).

In a time of cold religion and oppressive rules, Jesus' insights into God's law and character refreshed the weary. Christ's authentic walk with God contrasted with the stagnant lives of many religious leaders of the day. His compassion toward the unpopular and unattractive astonished people who were used to harsh judgment.

Jesus' miracles? Naturally, they produced surprise and elation. And both His crucifixion and resurrection, though unexpected and shocking, resulted in whispers of awe and shouts of freedom.

Today we still stand in awe of the Master. We're astonished at Jesus' ability to transform messed-up lives. We're humbled by His pity and love for us. We're simply amazed by His grace.

Heavenly Father, *I'm amazed not only by Your ability to save me from the penalty of my sins but by Your unconditional willingness to do so. By Your Son You have adopted me into Your family and given me Your indwelling Holy Spirit. I will stand amazed forever! Through Christ, amen.*

Perfect Obedience

Then he went down to Nazareth with them and was obedient to them (Luke 2:51).

Scripture: **Luke 2:51, 52**
Song: **"Lamb of God"**

What are those last words of reminder (or warning) so often uttered by parents before departing from their children? "Be good!"

Whether Mary and Joseph ever said these words to Jesus is unknown. One thing we do know: Our text records that Jesus was an obedient child.

Jesus' perfect childhood obedience, however, isn't just a nice little note in the Gospel text. That obedience was crucial to the plan of salvation. Without His having lived a perfect human life, Jesus would not have been qualified to serve as the unblemished lamb of God who would take away the sins of the world (see John 1:29).

Even at this early period in the life of Christ, the perfection that would be exchanged for the penalty of our sins was in full development. When Jesus died, He took our sins and gave us His righteous standing before God. When our heavenly Father sees us, He sees us as perfectly obedient sons and daughters. His obedience has become our obedience. It's the only way we could ever be good enough for Heaven.

Lord, *because You are good I am accounted good, though I know my daily life often shows otherwise. By Your grace may I strive to be in practice what I have already become in position. Through Christ, amen.*

Why Limit the Praise?

Praise him, sun and moon, praise him, all you shining stars (Psalm 148:3).

Scripture: **Psalm 148:1-6**
Song: **"Praise God from Whom All Blessings Flow"**

Mankind walking on the moon, rovers roaming the surface of Mars, and now an unmanned spacecraft on its way to Pluto—these are marvelous feats, but they only reach the outer fringes of one soloar system in God's vast universe.

Ever wonder why God created galaxies that no one may ever see? Perhaps it's simply because He can. When we stop to consider the seemingly infinite size of the universe, we realize how awesome and mighty its Creator must be. In Psalm 8:3, 4, King David says, "When I consider your heavens, the work of your fingers, the moon and the stars, which you have set in place, what is man that you are mindful of him?" A big universe proclaims a big God.

The enormous size of the universe also serves as a reminder of the limitlessness of God's attributes: His unlimited love, unlimited grace, and unlimited forgiveness for those who believe. Such infinite attributes remind us that God deserves . . . our unlimited praise.

Lord God of Creation, when I see the stars I am reminded of how big You are and how small I am in comparison. I acknowledge that You alone are the King of the Universe, and I invite You to make my soul, more and more, a territory fully conquered by Your loving reign. In the name of the Father, the Son, and the Holy Spirit, I pray. Amen.

No Fair?

Be still before the LORD and wait patiently for him; do not fret when men succeed in their ways, when they carry out their wicked schemes (Psalm 37:7).

Scripture: Psalm 37:1-11
Song: "Be Still and Know"

A big-rig truck driver was lying in his hospital bed, worried not about his recovery from a rollover but about how he would pay the hospital bill. His company refused to pay for his treatment. He was being held at fault for the accident caused by a load shift—even though he hadn't loaded the flatbed. More fines to pay and more points on his license. "It's not fair!" he shouted, startling the nurse working at his side. Here was the end of a career.

We all face an unfair life, in which ruthless and unprincipled people may well prosper while honest folk will suffer. Yet God's counsel to us is patience. Just be still and wait.

How hard to do! We want to "get back at them, and make them pay." But God says, "Wait." This approach will pay off—eventually—as a glimpse at the final verse of today's reading clearly reveals: "The meek will inherit the land and enjoy great peace." Let us trust God to right the wrongs, in His way, in His time.

O God, You are so gracious in the midst of an ungracious world. Thank You that judgment does not rest on our shoulders. In Jesus' name, amen.

January 7-13. **Charlotte Mize** has three published books and often speaks at retreats and seminars. She loves hiking in the mountains and doing needlework.

Stop That!

Do not hate your brother in your heart. Rebuke your neighbor frankly so you will not share in his guilt (Leviticus 19:17).

Scripture: **Leviticus 19:17, 18**
Song: **"Be Still, My Soul"**

Her 18-year-old stepbrother was headed for her younger brother with hatred in his eyes. Ten-year-old Jana stepped between them. "Don't hit him; he's little." Jason took another step closer, with Jana the first in line for a punch.

Hearing the ruckus, Jason's father rushed into the room. "Stop that!"

Jason halted, then whirled around and left the room. Jana was shaking. "Jana, you should have called me. You can't stop Jason by yourself," her stepfather said as he hugged both of the younger children.

The scene moved me to reflect: While trying to right the wrongs of the world, don't we often neglect to call upon the one who can save both us and our brothers from abuse? We may be called to rebuke the raging hater, but we must allow only our Father to chasten him. What a fine line between protecting the weak and usurping God's role! Thankfully, we can learn to let go of grudges and allow Him to fulfill—in His way and time—His promise: "It is mine to avenge; I will repay" (Romans 12:19).

Dear Father, *how like a child I act, rushing into Your role! Help me distinguish between standing up for the right and overstepping Your authority. For You alone are the only perfect judge. In Christ's name, amen.*

Good for Evil?

I tell you who hear me: Love your enemies, do good to those who hate you (Luke 6:27).

Scripture: **Luke 6:27, 28**
Song: **"I Love You with the Love of the Lord"**

Cindy questioned every decision I made. She clothed it as "constructive criticism," but it felt like insubordination. It was hard for me to lead a group of 12 support staff in our office, providing motivation, training, and encouragement to them. Cindy's constant carping undermined my confidence and leadership. I often heard secondhand complaints about her grumbling.

It was time for salary reviews. Our support staff was woefully underpaid, so I went to the CEO on their behalf. He asked whether I thought all of my staff people were working up to their potential. Here was my chance to let him know of Cindy's uncooperative spirit! Somehow, though, God stilled my voice, and I was able to recommend raises for all of them. Cindy never knew that her raise came because I went to bat for her.

It's hard to bless those who curse us. It's even more difficult to pray for them. I do pray for Cindy, since her work habits will no doubt land her in trouble some day. I also pray for myself, that I can love her in spite of my own hurt. After all, Jesus loves and blesses me, even when I fail Him.

Father, *it is because of Your Son's intercession for me that I am right with You. Help me learn to love as You love. Through Christ my Lord, amen.*

Above and Beyond

If someone strikes you on one cheek, turn to him the other also. If someone takes your cloak, do not stop him from taking your tunic (Luke 6:29).

Scripture: **Luke 6:29, 30**
Song: **"Is Your All on the Altar?"**

Have you ever been honored for going "above and beyond"? One company I worked for gave unexpected monetary awards to employees who performed well beyond their job descriptions. Of course, those extra tasks were usually done voluntarily and willingly. Still, it was nice to be recognized. And it was exciting to have senior management troop into one's office, smiling—and bearing an envelope with cash inside.

Jesus deals with a different situation: the times when we're coerced and mistreated. Even under duress we are to go above and beyond what is required of us. Under these circumstances, we will not be rewarded or even recognized—at least not by our tormentors! In fact, we may be ridiculed for being easy prey.

However, we are to yield willingly, offering more than is required. The reward comes not from those around us but from Jesus himself. He understands the stress we endure, and He recognizes our sacrifice. He too was coerced but willingly acquiesced for our benefit.

Father, life often requires more of me than I expect. Help me to look beyond my own "rights." May I willingly lay down my possessions to be generous, in Your name, even to those who exploit me. Through Jesus, amen.

Treat Them Right

Do to others as you would have them do to you (Luke 6:31).

Scripture: **Luke 6:31**
Song: **"Love One Another"**

Yesterday my husband came home irritated at the day's events. My child was angry with an apparently unfair world, and my mother complained about her arthritis acting up again.

Why don't they just get over it? I thought. Everybody has troubles, but I wish they wouldn't take it out on me.

Today I'm the one irritated, angry, and complaining. Without a word, my husband gives me a hug. My daughter offers to clean up the kitchen. My mother smiles and pats my cheek. All this kindness bothers me a bit. Why? Because they are treating me the way they wanted me to treat them the day before.

Often I would like to rewind the tape of life a couple of days. I would offer my husband a glass of iced tea and a quiet moment in his recliner. I would allow my child to vent his understandable frustrations in a safe environment. I would offer my mother a cup of hot cocoa and a gentle back rub.

But life doesn't rewind! I need to respond to opportunities as they arise—the privilege of simply treating others as I would like to be treated.

God, *forgive my impatience with family members. Help me feel their pain and respond in the same way I want them to respond to me. In this small way, let me be a servant in Your name. Through Christ I pray. Amen.*

Generosity

Love your enemies, do good to them, and lend to them without expecting to get anything back. Then your reward will be great, and you will be sons of the Most High, because he is kind to the ungrateful and wicked (Luke 6:35).

Scripture: **Luke 6:34-36**
Song: **"Let the Beauty of Jesus Be Seen in Me"**

We tend to think of generosity in connection with our friends or family. As usual, Jesus turns our thinking upside down: He expects us to be generous to our enemies.

First, then, we must identify whom we consider to be an enemy. Is it a coworker, a neighbor, a government agent, a foreigner, a wealthy oppressor? Then we must ask, "How can I be generous to this person?"

One way is simply to be liberal with forgiveness. What greater or more costly gift can we offer someone than our complete forgiveness, whether or not they request it? Another way is to supply what is lacking. If my adversary needs anything I can offer, Jesus tells me to provide it without expecting repayment. And how about imparting an unexpected kindness—a helping hand, a meal, a smile, or an encouraging word?

The supreme gift, though, is love. Can I sincerely love my enemy as I love my family or myself? If I can do that, I am truly reflecting the character of God. As His child, I have "inherited" His traits of kindness and mercy.

Dear Giver of Everything, *I want to emulate Your unconditional love. Help me see every enemy as a potential friend. In Jesus' name, amen.*

Ultimate Safety Net

The salvation of the righteous comes from the LORD; he is their stronghold in time of trouble (Psalm 37:39).

Scripture: **Psalm 37:35-40**
Song: **"You Are My Hiding Place"**

In 1989 a powerful earthquake shook San Francisco. Highways collapsed in tiers, sandwiching vehicles and drivers between layers of concrete. Buildings erupted in flames, sending firework-like embers skyward. Humanity poured out of downtown buildings, fleeing destruction.

It wasn't a good time for us to be visiting the city! Engulfed in a throng of commuters trying to get home, we didn't know the area well enough to navigate the interruptions in public transportation so we could return to our hotel many miles away. We were vulnerable to physical danger and to opportunists who might see a chance to exploit some naive out-of-towners.

After several hours of wandering the streets, we came upon a hotel employee who offered us a place to spend the night in the reinforced basement of his brand new hotel. We were safe once again.

Earthquake-like trials of life can assault us to the point that we become extremely vulnerable. The ruthless seem to flourish during these times, but we flounder. Yet God promises us a refuge during both physical and emotional upheavals. He alone is our place of ultimate safety.

Dear Father, *thank You for being my refuge in the time of trial. Help me let go of my self-sufficiency and turn only to You. In Jesus' name, amen.*

Shields Up!

The LORD is my strength and my shield; my heart trusts in him, and I am helped (Psalm 28:7).

Scripture: **Psalm 28:6-9**
Song: **"How Firm a Foundation"**

A starship glides gracefully through the eternal night of outer space. It passes through fields of stars, smearing streaks of light against the velvety blackness. All is serene. Without warning, an unseen enemy dives to the attack, pummeling the spacecraft with powerful lasers that could rip the ship in half. The seasoned crew reacts instantly, raising an invisible force field as thunderous explosions rock the craft.

It might be a scene from any science fiction movie. In reality, Christians are much like that starship crew sailing through the black night. Our unseen enemy lurks, watching for a vulnerable moment, seeking to exploit our weaknesses. He targets our lives, minds, and emotions. Yet an invisible force field surrounds believers with an impenetrable protection that also fortifies from within. Nothing can pass through the shield except that which our Father allows. He is stronger than every enemy and will see us through our dark night.

O Lord, You are El Shaddai, Almighty God, and there is no other like You. My heart sings for joy, knowing that no plan of Yours can be thwarted. Thank You for shielding me on every side. In Jesus' name, amen.

January 14–20. **Rhonda Brunea,** of Cherry Creek, New York, is a single mother of four. She loves reading and collecting amusing and fairly useless pets, like sheep.

Prodigal to Pray-er

One day Jesus was praying in a certain place. When he finished, one of his disciples said to him, "Lord, teach us to pray, just as John taught his disciples" (Luke 11:1).

Scripture: **Luke 11:1-4**
Song: **"He Knows"**

"Lying, stealing, gambling, novel-reading, licentiousness, extravagance, and almost every form of sin was indulged in by him," wrote biographer J. Gilchrist Lawson. "No one would have imagined that the sinful youth would ever become eminent for his faith in God and for his power in prayer."

Who was this miserable sinner? None other than the great nineteenth-century "prayer warrior" George Mueller—and that was before he went to jail for cheating an innkeeper out of a week's rent! In his own words, Mueller says of his youthful days: "I cared nothing for the Word of God."

Eventually, though, Mueller became known for never mentioning his needs to others; he laid everything before God with constant, patient intercession. And he kept precise records of his requests, to prove to the world that there is a God who hears His people.

Jesus had taught Mueller to pray. He will do the same for us, if we come to Him with an open heart, no matter the current state of our lives.

Lord, teach me to pray with a humble and contrite spirit, that those around me will see Your faithfulness when You answer. In Jesus' name, amen.

Be Bold

I tell you, though he will not get up and give him the bread because he is his friend, yet because of the man's boldness he will get up and give him as much as he needs (Luke 11:8).

Scripture: **Luke 11:5-8**
Song: **"Abba Father"**

Two girls wanted to go to the local mall one Saturday. "Let's ask my father," said one.

"Oh, no! He'll be angry," the second girl replied. The first girl was puzzled. "Why would he be angry with us, just for asking?"

"Well . . . what if he says no?" The second girl's voice quavered a little. Her friend shrugged her shoulders. "Then he says no. He does sometimes. So what? He'll say yes if he can."

We sometimes fear to ask our heavenly Father for the desires of our hearts, as if we're suspicious of His reaction. Will He strike us down if we ask with wrong motives? Will He be angry if we request something we don't really need? Will He answer no? (We don't always ask wisely, and sometimes the answer *ought* to be no.) But God invites us to ask boldly. He knows our motives are less than pure. Still He loves us. And can't we trust this wonderful Father to sort our imperfect prayers and do whatever is best?

My Abba, even the finest earthly father can't approach Your wisdom, patience, kindness, and love. Help me to keep my needs and desires before You, that our relationship might grow ever deeper. Through Christ, amen.

Too Easy?

Everyone who asks receives; he who seeks finds; and to him who knocks, the door will be opened (Luke 11:10).

Scripture: **Luke 11:9-12**
Song: **"Jesus Will Let You In"**

A woman stood in the darkness before the large, well-lit house. Snow encrusted the toes of her costly leather boots. She had been making her unsteady way home when someone told her about a great party at this house.

She was told, though, that she had to change her clothes to join this gathering. "I paid a lot of money for my outfit," she mumbled, watching a straggly teenaged girl knock and then boldly step over the threshold into the bright interior. She folded her arms around herself, indignant, and kicked the snow from her boots.

Laughter and music flooded into the street each time the door swung wide to admit another. She watched a white-robed woman gently assist a grimy man still reeling with drink. "They'll let *anybody* in there!" It was dark, and growing colder. The hour was late. She should go home and forget about these freaks. Still, those leaving the house looked so peaceful. It seemed too easy—knock, walk in, join the party. The woman frowned, and the worry lines marring her brow deepened.

Gracious Lord, may I never cease to wonder at Your wholehearted invitation to me—filthy rags and all. Thank You for clothing me in your righteousness through Your matchless grace. Please keep me alert to assist those still standing in the darkness. Through Christ I pray. Amen.

Someone's Daughter

I tell you the truth, anyone who will not receive the kingdom of God like a little child will never enter it (Luke 18:17).

Scripture: **Luke 18:1-17**
Song: **"Be Still, My Soul"**

Her world is crashing around her, but Rachel hardly notices. She is three years old, and she's known only deep love and protection. Blissfully unaware of the trauma rocking her mother, Rachel spins and twirls in a joyful dance choreographed by her trusting heart. The weary mother watches her daughter. "Like a child," she thinks.

Rachel has no worries. All will be well because Mommy is here. Mommy guards her from monsters in the night, comforts her when she's sad, and gives her everything she needs. Mommy is always there, and somehow she always knows just what to do.

If only that were true! The young woman's shoulders sag with the weight of it all. Bewildering fears and dire possibilities clutch her mind and drag her down into a swamp of confusion. "I can't do this," she thinks. Rachel twirls up to her mother, plants a warm kiss on her cheek, and then leaps away again, laughing. For a moment, the ache eases, and the young woman remembers that she, too, is Someone's daughter.

Father, help me remember that I am Your child. You love me with an ever-lasting love. You are always here, and always know what to do. I will dance with joy for such a Father. I will curl into Your strong arms and trust. I love You, my good Papa. In the name of Your Son, my Savior, I pray. Amen.

What a Great Day!

When the day of Pentecost came, they were all together in one place (Acts 2:1).

Scripture: **Luke 11:13; Acts 2:1-4**
Song: **"I've Got a River of Life"**

Behind a wall of shimmering heat, the lioness patiently stalks her prey—a large herd of antelope. There is strength in the unity of the herd, so she cannot attack them all at once. She might be trampled to death if she tried. She lurks until a single antelope strays from the safety of the herd. Only then does the lioness purr in anticipation of her feast. She crouches, gathering her strength for the chase, and launches her brutal attack.

The enemy of our souls also knows the power of unity. He seeks to divide in order to destroy us, one by one. Though each of us walks through life seemingly alone, no believer is ever truly alone. Our spirits gather at the Lord's table, and as we kneel before His glorious throne. Believers across the entire earth sing His praise as if from one throat.

Every follower of Jesus is part of a mighty fellowship that will never be broken. As our hearts gather in worship, His Spirit flows through us, and each of us is strengthened. All because of Pentecost, a great day indeed!

Dear Lord, thank You for sending Your Spirit to strengthen and encourage us until we all go Home. Help the family of believers always be all together in one place spiritually, so that You may work Your perfect plan through us. In the holy name of Jesus, my Lord and Savior, I pray. Amen.

Authentic Life

Blessed are they who maintain justice, who constantly do what is right (Psalm 106:3).

Scripture: **Psalm 106:1-3**
Song: **"Let Your Love Flow Through Me"**

Once there lived an influential man. At first glance, no one would think him a person of importance. He possessed only modest means, dressing neatly but with no great style. He lived quietly in a humble home with a sweet-tempered wife, and he never did anything extraordinary. Yet when the man passed away, people came by the hundreds to pay their respects to his widow.

"Your husband was a good man," someone said. "I was in trouble once, and he was the only one to help me."

"I respected your husband more than anyone I've ever met," said another. "I don't remember ever hearing him speak an unkind word about anyone."

Another commented with a puzzled look, "He always seemed so peaceful, even when I knew he had troubles of his own." And one woman approached the widow with tears pooling in her eyes. "I always wanted to ask . . . what made your husband so different?"

To all these the widow smiled and replied, "My husband had a wise and faithful Friend. Come to our home this Sunday. I'll introduce you." And she did.

Dear Lord, *I ask that Your sweet fragrance saturate my life and draw seekers closer to You. Help me love You above all and live authentically for the sake of those who are watching. Thank You, in Jesus' name. Amen.*

Supposed Friends

Free me from the trap that is set for me, for you are my refuge. Into your hands I commit my spirit; redeem me, O Lord, the God of truth (Psalm 31:4, 5).

Scripture: **Psalm 31:1-5**
Song: **"A Shield About Me"**

It seems strange now, but many years ago I found myself under surveillance as a scientist in a large company. The secret observation wasn't for something I had done but because of someone who worked in the laboratory with me. The young man had a family, a job, and was going to school at night to do even better. I often wondered how he had enough energy to do everything. One day the police came and took him away.

A comment he made a few days earlier struck me: "I shouldn't have trusted my supposed friends; they just used me." I later discovered that his friends were making and selling illegal drugs.

Psalm 31 is a study in contrasts. There is evil around us in the world and in people's hearts; we can get trapped. In contrast, there is the Lord, God of truth and love. Jesus entered this world of lies and deceit, but in dying He preached the message of a father He could trust—"Father, into your hands I commit my spirit" (Luke 23:46).

Lord, I am so thankful that in You there is no deception. I commit my whole life into Your hands. All praise to You, in Christ's name. Amen.

January 21–27. **Daniel F. Varnell** is a part-time scientist and a church worker. He loves spending time with his wife and daughters, playing golf, and cooking chili.

Of Great Worth

Consider the ravens: They do not sow or reap, they have no storeroom or barn; yet God feeds them. And how much more valuable you are than birds! (Luke 12:24).

Scripture: **Luke 12:22-24**
Song: **"O the Deep, Deep Love of Jesus"**

My children love our young cat. They feed, hug, and spoil him constantly. So when he was about to die this past year, we had a very sad household. My wife and I spent a fairly large amount of money to save him. He was worth it—because he was loved.

Jesus told His disciples not to worry. Yet I still find that at times my mind is weighed down. Worries sneak in on me from all kinds of insecurities—like when I'm approaching my yearly performance appraisal at work.

Jesus started His teaching on worry with the key to breaking free. The key is our worth, our value, in God's eyes. Each and every one of us is a great and precious joy to God. If I provided an operation for a family cat, how much more will my heavenly Father take care of me?

And, of course, worry is mostly just a pure waste of emotional energy. As one anonymous quipster once put it: "Don't tell me that worry doesn't do any good. I know better; the things I worry about *never* happen."

Heavenly Father, *I accept the truth of Your Word that You love and care for me deeply. Let my burdens fall from my shoulders this day. Let my anxious thoughts be replaced by thoughts of Your care. Thank You, Lord, for Your great and awesome love. I pray through my deliverer, Jesus. Amen.*

Always a Majority

Who of you by worrying can add a single hour to his life? Since you cannot do this very little thing, why do you worry about the rest? (Luke 12:25, 26).

Scripture: **Luke 12:25, 26**
Song: **"Breathe"**

I read the other day that the word *worry* comes from an old Anglo-Saxon word meaning "to strangle or choke." In my teens I woke one night unable to breathe because my sinuses and lungs were congested. After several minutes of gasping for air, I came through those scary moments, with the help of my parents. However, a deep worry filled my mind for years.

And, recently, after pushing myself and taking on too many commitments, I started having panic attacks. My throat would tighten up, and I worried about breathing. Apparently the old fear was still there.

Jesus taught that worry can't add anything to our lives, not even an hour. Yet, for God to add an hour is a simple thing. And for God to help us move through any tough circumstance—could that ever be too hard for Him?

As I have meditated upon the truths in these Scriptures about worry, I have felt my worries disappear. As the old saying goes: "Me plus God always equals a majority."

Dear Heavenly Father, *I praise You for Your awesome power. Since nothing is too hard for You, let me not be anxious but at peace, knowing that my life is in Your infinitely capable hands. I pray this prayer in the name of Jesus, my merciful Savior and Lord. Amen.*

Growing Beautiful

Consider the lilies, how they grow: they neither toil nor spin; and yet I say to you, even Solomon in all his glory was not arrayed like one of these (Luke 12:27, *New King James Version*).

Scripture: Luke 12:27, 28
Song: "How Beautiful"

Every year I plant flower seeds, and they turn into beautiful, blossoming plants. It amazes me—all of that beauty lies within every tiny seed. The seeds had no say about how they'd be planted, nor the soil they would inhabit, nor how well (or not!) I might care for them. Nor did the seeds produce their own beauty from scratch. God had already placed that potential within them.

What of us? Jesus said we must fall to the ground and die spiritually (John 12:24), be born again of the Spirit (John 3:3), and grow into the image of Jesus Christ (Ephesians 4:15). These things don't arise from our natural humanity or come about by self-effort; they are all of God, all of His grace.

It's true that we are made in the image of God, thus we have intelligence, personality, and will inherent within us. But the ability to save ourselves by "toiling" always escapes us. Like the lilies, if we are to grow beautiful in God's sight, it must be His work alone.

Father, You are at work conforming me to the beautiful likeness of Your Son, Jesus. Day by day, let me rely upon Your grace, being confident of this very thing, that He who has begun a good work in me will complete it until the day of Jesus Christ. In His name, amen.

God Gave Favor

Seek the kingdom of God, and all these things shall be added to you (Luke 12:31, *New King James Version*).

Scripture: **Luke 12:29-31**
Song: **"God Is Good"**

There just wasn't enough time each week in my schedule to do all I wanted for God, so I decided to try to work three days as a scientist instead of five. I fasted and prayed. My wife agreed. Then doors opened, I found favor where there usually was none, and my request was approved. My pay and pension were cut accordingly.

The following year, the company I worked for announced that there would be no raises. God then extended more grace. You see, even though I was only working part time in a competitive field, I was given a promotion. It included a raise. Even better, with the promotion to a higher position I was considered *underpaid* —and was therefore exempt from the ban on raises! I received a second raise. As far as I can tell, God wonderfully made up a large part of what I gave up for Him. And I was able to keep blessing others in His name.

During those days, I learned a lot about seeking God's kingdom and His will for my life. As the writer of Hebrews wrote, "He is a rewarder of those who diligently seek Him" (11:6).

*O, **Wondrous God**, thank You for blessing Your servant. You have given me great joy in serving You. Help me remember Your goodness as I reach out to others in Your name. Through Christ, I pray. Amen.*

God Said a Thousand

Do not be afraid, little flock, for your Father has been pleased to give you the kingdom (Luke 12:32).

Scripture: **Luke 12:32-34**
Song: **"He's Got the Whole World in His Hands"**

Not long after I truly trusted my life to Jesus, a visiting missions organizer came to our church. He began speaking in general about missions and then, surprisingly, talked at great length about the needs in one of the former states of the Soviet Union. Two members of the church volunteered to go and preach the gospel there. The only thing that remained was the money to send them. God impressed on my heart to give a thousand dollars towards the trip.

Never had I conceived of giving such a large amount to anything! I was reluctant to tell my dear wife. On the way home, though, I tentatively suggested we give substantially to the trip—"maybe several hundred dollars."

Oh, how foolish I was! My wife replied, "I felt God would have us give a thousand dollars."

I learned a lesson, and I'm still learning. We shouldn't be afraid of giving what God asks for, or of talking about it with our spouses. After all, God has already given us the kingdom.

Heavenly Father, how great is Your wisdom and how generous You are toward me. I know I am not very wise about using the resources You have provided, but I pray that in the days ahead You will lead me to treasure Your kingdom deeply and give more generously. In Jesus' name, amen.

Which Airline?

Do not put your trust in princes, in mortal men, who cannot save. When their spirit departs, they return to the ground; on that very day their plans come to nothing (Psalm 146:3, 4).

Scripture: **Psalm 146:1-7**
Song: **"People Get Ready"**

At the airport, Billy was surprised to have a choice of airlines. The first airline had a sleek plane, offered champagne, hundreds of movies, and good-looking attendants. Royalty, too, was traveling on the flight.

The other airline offered just basic amenities with a smile. They did say the owner and maker of the plane would be with them. And Billy noted their guarantee to get him to his destination safely and on time. Surely, Billy thought, the other plane would do the same. "Hurry up. This is the fun flight," said the man at the fancy airline. Billy quickly got on board.

The rich food left him sick. The movies became annoying. His seat was unreasonably small. Then Billy felt strange. They were losing altitude. He saw the pilot shoot past as his parachute opened. His heart sank. In the distance he saw the other plane. Everyone was smiling. A confident man sat in their midst.

Yes, a fictional scenario. But I am glad my destination is eternal and wonderful. Jacob's God, the God of truth, is also my God. May each person choose wisely his path!

Heavenly Father, *today, let my focus be on You and not the things and troubles of this world. I pray this prayer in Jesus' name. Amen.*

Family Faith

We will not hide them from their children; we will tell the next generation the praiseworthy deeds of the LORD (Psalm 78:4).

Scripture: **Psalm 78:1-4**
Song: **"God of Our Fathers"**

I knew that my mother's family had been Christians for several generations. When I began to explore the history of her family, though, I discovered the true extent.

In 1662, John Argor, one of my mother's ancestors and a Cambridge educated vicar, refused to sign the Uniformity Act. The Act required all ministers to approve the Book of Common Prayer and to acknowledge the unlawfulness of taking up arms against the king.

Argor lost his pulpit, and friends asked him how he thought he would provide for his large family. To this he answered, "God is my housekeeper, and I believe He will provide for us."

Mom never told me this story, but she lived a faithful life herself. When she developed cancer, her life and writings were an inspiration to many. After her death, one of her articles was published. She wrote that she thanked God for allowing her to have cancer because of the lessons she had learned from the experience.

Father, *thank You for our children and grandchildren. Help us to share Jesus and our faith stories with the next generation. In Jesus' name, amen.*

January 28–31. **Rosalie Yoakam** is a freelance writer and a columnist for the Dayton Daily News. She and her husband, Bill, live in Springboro, Ohio.

On a Quest

He said to them, "Take nothing for your journey, neither a staff, nor a bag, nor bread, nor money; and do not even have two tunics apiece" (Luke 9:3, *New American Standard Bible*).

Scripture: **Luke 9:1-10**
Song: **"Leaving All to Follow Jesus"**

My husband, Bill, was nearing graduation from college. I was the current breadwinner, teaching elementary school. As I came in from school, Bill met me. "We're going to Findlay," he said. "They just posted a job opening for assistant city engineer."

We jumped into our old car and drove the 50 miles. Two blocks from the city engineer's office our car stalled and refused to restart. A mechanic from a nearby garage jump-started the engine, but it cost $5, all the money we had between us.

The vehicle quit again. A kind stranger pushed our disabled auto for several blocks, and then into a service station. The verdict was a bad fuel pump.

We walked five blocks to the local minister's house. His wife fed us, and then they took us back to the station, where they paid for the repairs (money we repaid later).

Bill left a note on the closed engineer's office door. But a few weeks later Bill was appointed Assistant City Engineer of Findlay, Ohio.

Dear Father in Heaven, *thank You for providing what I need as I journey through life intent upon bringing glory to Your name. In the name of the Father, the Son, and the Holy Spirit, amen.*

Postal Moment

Go your ways; behold, I send you out as lambs in the midst of wolves (Luke 10:3, *New American Standard Bible*).

Scripture: **Luke 10:1-3**
Song: **"Anywhere with Jesus"**

I was going postal. An acquaintance had hired me to teach workshops for her company. My job was to instruct attendees on how to obtain a high score on the postal exam. I had no experience with such tests, but had been trained . . . over the phone.

Preparing for the first class, because I felt insecure, I typed out everything I was to say. Before the first session, I placed the notes on the podium and went to the hallway to greet the participants.

As I collected money from the students, a competitor slipped into the classroom, stole my notes, and left. When I discovered the loss, I was terrified. However, in spite of my panic, I managed to teach the first class successfully. In fact, my presentation from memory was perhaps more effective than a rote reading from notes. It was a learning experience for me as well as the students.

I learned Jesus not only sends His little lambs among wolves. He protects them while they are there.

Dear Father, thank You for protecting me as I go about my days. I am sometimes tempted to think that parts of my life are too small for Your attention. But remind me that You are with me in the midst of every moment. Help me to rest in Your unchanging care this day and every day. In the name of Your precious Son, my Savior, I pray. Amen.

Peace for Troubled Households

Whatever house you enter, first say, "Peace be to this house" (Luke 10:5, *New American Standard Bible*).

Scripture: **Luke 10:4-7**
Song: **"Peace, Perfect Peace"**

Westin, one of my first graders, was the picture of health, stocky, with dark eyes and hair. But at the beginning of the school year his mother recounted his history. Westin had developed leukemia at age three. He must go to a clinic for periodic tests.

Tearfully, she reported at mid-year: the leukemia had returned. Westin would undergo chemotherapy and be unable to attend school.

In order to continue his educational progress, I agreed to tutor the boy in his home. Once a week, after teaching a full day, I went to Westin's small white house. Before exiting the car each week, I prayed for his strength and peace.

His treatment was lengthy, lasting well into his second year. His second-grade teacher took over the tutoring until he was able to rejoin his class.

Ten years later, both teachers were invited to an anniversary party to rejoice over Westin's prolonged remission from disease. We were thrilled to celebrate with the joyful family. And I was reminded: Christian service, with compassion, brings peace to troubled households.

Dear Father, I pray for the peace of my friends and neighbors. May I serve them with Your compassion. In Jesus' name. Amen.

DEVOTIONS

Gary Allen, Editor

O my people, hear my teaching . . . tell the next generation the praiseworthy deeds of the LORD.

—Psalm 78:1a, 4b

FEBRUARY

Photo © Jupiterimages

© 2007 STANDARD PUBLISHING, 8121 Hamilton Avenue, Cincinnati, Ohio, 45231, a division of STANDEX INTERNATIONAL Corporation. Topics based on the Home Daily Bible Readings, International Sunday School Lessons. © 2003 by the Committee on the Uniform Series. Printed in the U.S.A. All Scripture quotations, unless otherwise indicated, are taken from the HOLY BIBLE, NEW INTERNATIONAL VERSION®. NIV®. Copyright © 1973, 1978, 1984 by International Bible Society. Used by permission of Zondervan. All rights reserved. Where noted, Scripture quotations are from the following, used with permission of the copyright holders, all rights reserved: King James Version *(KJV)*. New American Standard Bible *(NASB)*, © The Lockman Foundation, 1960, 1962, 1963, 1968, 1971, 1972, 1973, 1975, 1977, 1995. The Revised Standard Version of the Bible *(RSV)*, copyrighted 1946, 1952, © 1971, 1973. Contemporary English Version *(CEV)*, 1991, 1992, 1995 American Bible Society.

Welcome Food

Whatever city you enter, and they receive you, eat what is set before you (Luke 10:8, *New American Standard Bible*).

Scripture: Luke 10:8-12
Song: "Break Thou the Bread of Life"

In Rostov, Russia, we met a woman who said she knew it was possible to live on just bread and salt. She had done so for a period of time during WW II. The same woman thanked my husband and me for the care packages she had received from America following the war. She credited the food contained in those packages for her survival.

Have you noticed how sharing a meal produces an atmosphere where intimate fellowship can develop? Our conversation took place in 1992 in the elderly woman's house, one of the few buildings in her neighborhood to endure the battle that once raged in her city. As we sat at her dining room table, her story was interpreted by her daughter, Lydia, an English teacher.

The events the Russian lady recalled had taken place many years before, but she had lacked the opportunity to show her gratitude. She now eagerly served a meal to the first Americans she had met since that time.

The borscht soup was delicious. And how our gracious host smiled when my husband asked for seconds!

Father, thank You for blessing me with memories of hospitality, times when I have shared food, and Your love, with others. In Jesus' name. Amen.

February 1–3. **Rosalie Yoakam** is a freelance writer and a columnist for the *Dayton Daily News*. She and her husband, Bill, live in Springboro, Ohio.

The Heavenly Register

Do not rejoice in this, that the spirits are subject to you, but rejoice that your names are recorded in heaven (Luke 10:20, *New American Standard Bible*).

Scripture: **Luke 10:17-20**
Song: **"When the Roll Is Called Up Yonder"**

My college diploma sits proudly on the shelf above my computer. It is precious to me because it took me 25 years to earn it. After high school, I completed two years of college and then dropped out of the academic scene. I married, had three daughters, and thought I would never be able to finish my education.

The Lord had other plans. When a Christian school was established in our congregation, the director asked whether I could renew my teaching license. I contacted a local college and found it was possible. Wilmington College accepted my previous credits and worked out a plan for the completion of my course of study.

Today, my name is listed as a recipient of the Bachelor of Arts degree. What a great day of celebration when I graduated! My dream had finally come true.

We will all "graduate" from this earth some day, entering an existence beyond the grave. If we're recorded on the heavenly register, what a far greater event than any other commencement day!

Dear Father, *thank You for loving me, forgiving me, and enrolling me for a heavenly eternity in fellowship with You. I am so grateful to be Your child. In the name of Jesus, Lord and Savior of all, I pray. Amen.*

Awesome Deeds

Come and see the works of God, Who is awesome in His deeds toward the sons of men (Psalm 66:5, *New American Standard Bible*).

Scripture: **Psalm 66:5-12**
Song: **"In the Hour of Trial"**

Charity Lynch was a Quaker woman who moved with her husband and children to Ohio from South Carolina in the early 1800s. They settled in the town of Waynesville and were very happy there— until tragedy struck in 1813. Their newborn son died. The husband's death soon followed. Then Charity herself fell ill and was not expected to live. The Lynchs' seven surviving children were distributed to six different homes in four towns.

When Charity was told that her children were gone, she could only accept it as a temporary arrangement. She was determined to get them back. Slowly her health returned, and she was able to write about how she dealt with this time of intense tribulation:

"At that time I often retired to my room, shut the door, took my Bible, walked my room, and read some consoling promise of the gospel. I often was able to rejoice in the midst of grief, those days when I lived only for my dear children. For them my daily prayer was offered up to the throne of grace."

She eventually regained all her children.

*Thank You, **Father**, for Your awesome love and care. In the midst of the most difficult times, keep me close! In Jesus' name I pray. Amen.*

The Night Meditation

On my bed I remember you; I think of you through the watches of the night (Psalm 63:6).

Scripture: **Psalm 63:1-6**
Song: **"The Morning Light Is Breaking"**

Unlike my seatmate who was asleep before the plane left the runway, I couldn't get comfortable. Whenever I closed my eyes, all I could think about was the reason I was making this trip.

The night before, I'd been surrounded by friends traveling behind a horse-drawn sleigh, listening to the sleigh bells and the sounds of horses' hoofs as they crunched through the crusty snow. Now, one night later, my thoughts were troubled as I took the overnight flight to be with my daughter who was facing a lengthy surgical procedure to eradicate cancer. Alone, with no one to talk with, I felt tears threatening to spill down my cheeks. But in the silence I also recalled a hymn I'd learned as a child, "Anywhere with Jesus I can safely go."

Whether we're facing illness, difficult times, or searing loneliness, we are invited to meditate on God's love. In the long night hours He reaches through the darkness to remind us we are never alone.

O God, thank You for reminding me that I am never alone in this life. Help me to recollect Your abiding presence regularly, especially in the times when I'm most tempted to worry. Thank You, in Jesus' name. Amen.

February 4–10. **Elaine Ingalls Hogg,** of New Brunswick, Canada is a speaker and author, having written two books and several hundred devotionals and articles.

He Went First

This is he that was spoken of by the prophet Esaias, saying, The voice of one crying in the wilderness, Prepare ye the way of the Lord, make his paths straight (Matthew 3:3, *King James Version*).

Scripture: **Matthew 3:1-6**
Song: **"Prepare the Way, O Zion!"**

"I'm scared."

I'm not exactly sure how old I was when I first uttered those words, but I do remember the circumstances with certainty. I wanted to go with my dad, but the tide was out, and his boat looked so low in the water. And I'd never climbed down a ladder before.

"I'll go first," Dad said. "I'll guide where to put your feet. All you have to do is take one step at a time and hang on." So Dad stood on the ladder, and I backed onto the first rung. Now, instead of seeing the distance to the bobbing boat below, all I saw was my father's arms around me, surrounding me, protecting me from falling, directing my footsteps onto each successive rung.

As John prepared the way for Jesus, so Jesus has gone ahead of us to prepare the way to Heaven. Why look into the distance to see all the obstacles on our journey? Instead, we can visualize His protecting arms around us and hear His gentle voice directing our way. "I'll go first," He says. And He did—at the cross.

Lord, thank You for sending Jesus ahead of me to the grave, eternally defeating Death for all who follow Him. Praise to You, in His name! Amen.

Bringing Good News

After John was put in prison, Jesus went into Galilee, pro-claiming the good news of God (Mark 1:14).

Scripture: Mark 1:14, 15
Song: "Victory in Jesus"

Shortly after my daughter finished her treatments for cancer, she ran a marathon. The act of simply completing the run symbolized a great personal victory.

Historians tell us the first marathon run took place in 490 BC, when a soldier named Pheidippides ran with news from a battlefield on the plain of Marathon to the city of Athens. After a three-hour run of more than 25 miles, Pheidippides died of exhaustion—but not before he delivered this momentous message to his country's citizens: "Nike! (We conquer!)"

Pheidippides was so excited about the Greeks' victory over the Persians that he gave everything he had to tell others the good news. We too have news to share: "Jesus Christ brings victory!"

Christ died on the cross and rose again, defeating Satan and conquering death. As Christians, we have been given good news—no, better than good news. We've been given the best news of all time. Jesus Christ has paid the penalty for our sin. When we tell others of this marvelous victory, should we give less than our all?

Dear God, impress upon me the magnitude of the news Your Son, Jesus, brought to our world. Help me to give my all so that others will know of this great victory. In the precious name of Jesus, I pray. Amen.

Staying in Tune?

I tell you, no! But unless you repent, you too will all perish (Luke 13:5).

Scripture: **Luke 13:1-5**
Song: **"Repent, the Kingdom Draweth Nigh"**

When I was taking piano lessons, my teacher always tried to make the instruction more appealing by telling me facts about the composers I was studying. One day we were working through a piece by Handel, and she told me of a time when Handel became impatient with one of the singers in his choir. Apparently, the chorister continued to sing his own unusual interpretations instead of following the maestro's instructions. Handel supposedly took the offending member by the legs and hung him by the heels out of a third-story window! Finally, the chorister repented and agreed to sing in the maestro's way.

Unlike Handel, God doesn't take us by the heels and hold us upside down until we agree to follow Him. Nonetheless, if we are to find peace and harmony in our lives, we will surely be led to times of repentance. This means not only saying we are sorry and asking God to forgive us for our sin. It also calls for making a 180-degree turn away from sin. Thereafter, we will intend to walk in a different direction, relying on the Spirit to keep us steady, strong, and in tune with the Maestro of our days.

Dear God, as I look back through the days of my life, I can see where I have been guilty of rebelling against Your will and Your ways. I'm sorry. From now on, I want to do things Your way. Through Christ, amen.

One More Chance!

"Sir," the man replied, "leave it alone for one more year, and I'll dig around it and fertilize it. If it bears fruit next year, fine! If not, then cut it down" (Luke 13:8, 9).

Scripture: **Luke 13:6-9**
Song: **"The Water of Life"**

There's nothing like watching a living thing grow, even as the cold blasts of winter close in all around us. A few years ago I bought an amaryllis bulb to plant. According to the instructions, I needed to give the bulb a good soaking and then water it only once a week until a green shoot would appear.

All through the month of February I watered and watched. "This thing is never going to grow!" I exclaimed after watering it for the fourth week in a row and finding no sign of life. "I should throw it out."

In the end I decided to water and fertilize it one more time, thus giving it a last chance to show some sign of life. Although slow starting, with the right amount of moisture and fertilizer, the plant grew and produced a beautiful flower.

When we allow the Master to care for us in all His loving ways, we can grow and bring forth fruit. He doesn't give up on us. He patiently lets us make our mistakes or just lie dormant until we've had enough of our lonely living apart from Him. Then, watch us grow!

God, *bring forth the kind of fruits in me that demonstrate my roots go deep in Your love. Be the master gardner of my life, in Christ's name. Amen.*

Turn from Danger

I preached that they should repent and turn to God and prove their repentance by their deeds (Acts 26:20).

Scripture: **Acts 26:19-23**
Song: **"Repent! 'Tis the Voice of Jesus"**

Nineteen-year-old Jeff was part of a work team that went out from our church to help the victims of Hurricane Katrina in 2005. Upon his return, he told of his experiences.

Fighting back tears, he said, "When I met Don in a church parking lot, he was volunteering to help the flood victims. Although a young man like me, he'd already served jail time and had lost touch with his family.

"During the hurricane he'd found shelter in one of the few churches not already flooded. In the early morning hours, staring at the cross at the front of the church, he repented of his sins and turned to God. So complete was the change in his life that he called his family, asking for their forgiveness and reconciliation. Now, instead of being guarded in a prison cell, he was acting as a security guard at the distribution center."

Don's deeds—helping others, being trustworthy—proved his true repentance. Thankfully, God saves us while we are still *un*worthy. But He doesn't leave us in our sad state. He invites us into a brand new lifestyle.

Dear God, *I know others see You through how I conduct my life. Help me to proclaim Your matchless mercy by my life of gratefulness and good works. Through Christ my Savior, I pray. Amen.*

Can't Earn Heaven

For the LORD watches over the way of the righteous, but the way of the wicked will perish (Psalm 1:6).

Scripture: **Psalm 1**
Song: **"Each Step I Take"**

The peace of a beautiful summer afternoon was shattered by the unmistakable sound of a man's voice crying out, *"Help!"* Someone was in danger. My heart raced as I ran to dial 9-1-1. "There's a man in the lake," I said. "He's calling for help."

"Can you tell me where you live?" the voice on the other end of the line asked. Struggling to stay calm so I could give clear directions, I said, "West Bay. Please hurry!" I went on to explain, "When you get to Cleveland there's a fork in the road. Be sure to take the road on the right because the sign marked West Bay Road doesn't actually lead to West Bay." I explained further . . .

If the emergency crew had gone the wrong way, someone could have perished. Today's psalm speaks of the moral decisions we need to make during our lifetimes. Ultimately, they are matters of life and death. Should we choose the path of our own righteousness, we will fall short of eternal life. If we choose God alone as our righteousness, we will enjoy wonderful fellowship with His Son in this life—and enjoy Heaven with Him thereafter. What a loving and gracious Lord is ours!

Dear God, help me to listen closely to Your instructions that I might stay on the path of righteousness this day. Through my Lord Christ. Amen.

Egg on My Face

He guides the humble in what is right and teaches them his way (Psalm 25:9).

Scripture: **Psalm 25:1-10**
Song: **"More Like the Master"**

I was wrestling with a computer problem, but the computer was winning. "Let me show you how this works," said my husband, who seemed to be getting a little frustrated with me. He made a number of suggestions, some of which I'd already tried without success; others, I just didn't think would work. In desperation, though, I finally swallowed my pride and listened carefully to his instructions.

Click. Click. Click. Problem solved.

This is known as "egg on my face time."

I'm sure God must shake His head when we insist on doing things our own way. We think we know the best way to handle a situation, but He can see the whole picture from beginning to end. After making a mess of things, we end up crying out for Him to rescue us. He graciously steps in, guiding us and teaching us His ways when we're finally ready to accept His direction.

Our pride can be the biggest barrier to our relationship with the Lord. It takes a humble attitude to receive truth.

Father, thank You for Your patience when I'm in an I-can-do-it-myself mode. You whisper to my heart through Your Word until I get the message. Praise to You, in the name of Jesus! Amen.

February 11–17. **Susan J. Reinhardt** is an office manager and writer who enjoys antiquing. She and her husband live in Souderton, Pennsylvania.

Watching for a Mistake

One Sabbath, when Jesus went to eat in the house of a prominent Pharisee, he was being carefully watched (Luke 14:1).

Scripture: **Luke 14:1-6**
Song: **"Jesus Is Passing This Way"**

In sixth grade, one of my classmates, Judy, was a top-notch student. I wanted to be the best, but the result was always the same: Judy came out number one, while I was the runner-up. The green-eyed monster of jealousy grabbed my heart. I avoided her like the plague.

Did I seize the opportunity to be challenged, learn from her successes, and develop a friendship with her? No. I became upset with her and swirled down into self-pity.

The Pharisees had Jesus right there with them, eating a meal with Him. He spoke to them, encouraging them to look at life through the lens of God's love and concern for a sick man. Yet they allowed pride, jealousy, and a know-it-all attitude to rob them of blessing. Instead of seeing what they could learn, they secretly watched to find some fault or weakness.

It takes a humble heart to rejoice with others. On the other hand, the Germans have a word, *schadenfreude,* meaning to "rejoice in the misfortunes of others." We have that option too. But why not choose to learn from others' mistakes—and celebrate with them in their successes?

Lord, may I recognize You as the source of my strength and ability. Therefore, let me be thankful for the successes in my own life and in the lives of others. All the glory goes to You alone. In Jesus' name, amen.

SPS!

When someone invites you to a wedding feast, do not take the place of honor, for a person more distinguished than you may have been invited (Luke 14:8).

Scripture: **Luke 14:7-9**
Song: **"I Need Thee Every Hour"**

When I was growing up, Mom tried to instill certain strong values in me. For example, she wouldn't allow bragging. Whenever I showed any signs of self-aggrandizement, she would comment, "SPS," which stood for "self-praise stinks." While she was lavish with her praise of my accomplishments and abilities, she didn't hesitate to correct me if I was becoming obnoxious.

Jesus' words usually fly in the face of human wisdom. We're told it's a dog-eat-dog world, so we have to compete aggressively and push ourselves into the limelight. But Jesus spoke of handling the everyday experiences of life with humility and grace. He told people not to grab the best seats for themselves but to take a lower place. He pointed out how embarrassing it would be if someone told them to give up their hard-won place of privilege for an even more favored guest.

Giving ourselves honor leaves us unfulfilled—and constantly vulnerable to being "taken down a peg." How much sweeter our reward when it comes by pure grace!

Father, when I'm tempted to grab position or honor, help me to remember that self-praise ends in meager satisfaction. Let me find my joy in honoring You with a servant heart. In the precious name of Jesus I pray. Amen.

Parade for . . . Whom?

Everyone who exalts himself will be humbled, and he who humbles himself will be exalted (Luke 14:11).

Scripture: **Luke 14:10, 11**
Song: **"Have Thy Way, Lord"**

In the book of Esther, Haman enjoyed great power in the king's court. Instead of being thankful, though, he longed for honor and praise. Therefore, when godly Mordecai refused to "bow and scrape" before him, Haman raged.

One day, Mordecai discovered a plot against the king, notified the authorities, and thereby saved the king's life. Mordecai didn't demand any recognition; he just went about his business. Later, however, when the king came across the account of Mordecai's good deed, he was disturbed to find this courageous whistle-blower hadn't been properly rewarded.

The king called Haman and asked him what he would do for a great man. Haman assumed the king was talking about him and suggested the equivalent of our ticker-tape parade. You can imagine Haman's shock and humiliation when the king commanded him to do all these things for Mordecai!

Someone once said, "The way up is down." If you try to set up your own ticker-tape parade, you'll likely find you've prepared it for someone else.

Father, thank You for Your many blessings. Help me to remember that true promotion and favor come only from You. In Jesus' name, amen.

No Strings Attached

When you give a banquet, invite the poor, the crippled, the lame, the blind, and you will be blessed. Although they cannot repay you, you will be repaid at the resurrection of the righteous (Luke 14:13, 14).

Scripture: **Luke 14:12-14**
Song: **"Jesus Is All the World to Me"**

A mom smiles as a server puts a scoop of mashed potatoes on her child's plate. An elderly man happily chats with people at his table, glad for the company. A woman in a wheelchair is thankful she can get out of the house.

The server's back aches from hours of preparation. Her family has sacrificed their own traditions to be here. None of these people will ever invite her for dinner at their homes. Yet, her heart overflows with joy as their faces radiate hope for the future.

Jesus told His hosts not to invite their friends, relatives, or rich neighbors in hopes that they'd reciprocate in turn. Instead, He instructed them to extend hospitality to those who had no way of repaying. Such hosts would be blessed and honored by God on the day when He puts all things right.

Giving "with no strings attached" can produce great joy in our hearts. Whatever it costs us in time, money, and effort to serve the poor is far outweighed by the delight it brings to God's heart.

Heavenly Father, *give me a heart filled with compassion and love for those who can't repay the kindness You call me to share. In Jesus' name, amen.*

Credit Where It's Due

Whereof I was made a minister, according to the gift of the grace of God given unto me by the effectual working of his power. Unto me, who am less than the least of all saints, is this grace given, that I should preach among the Gentiles the unsearchable riches of Christ (Ephesians 3:7, 8, *King James Version*).

Scripture: **Ephesians 3:1-10**
Song: **"Cleanse Me"**

As a world-renowned preacher stepped up to the pulpit, the crowd gave him its full attention, waiting for profound words of wisdom. Yet he spoke with great simplicity and humility. Afterwards, a reporter said to him, "Dr. Smith, you have a seminary degree and several doctorates. You've traveled the world and met many great leaders. How does it feel to be so honored?"

The preacher smiled and said, "I'm nothing special. Jesus Christ is the source of my abilities."

This man, like Paul, refused to rely on his heritage or academic background for his effectiveness in ministry. He stressed God's grace in his life, recognizing the ministry as a gifting from God. He was more interested in presenting the gospel than building his reputation.

We can be thankful for men and women like this, who serve the church with pure hearts. They simply give credit where *all* the credit is due.

Father, when I'm tempted to bask in applause, remind me that it's You who have extended blessing. Keep working through me, in Jesus' name. Amen.

Key Element of Change

All of you, clothe yourselves with humility toward one another, because, "God opposes the proud but gives grace to the humble" (1 Peter 5:5).

Scripture: **1 Peter 5:1-5**
Song: **"I Surrender All"**

Her dad had abandoned Liza and her mom before her birth. Further complicating matters, her mom's family rejected them as well. As an adult, Liza was drawn to a lifestyle of partying and drinking. Several failed marriages and ill health left her a broken, addicted, suicidal woman.

But Liza's story has a happy ending. She discovered a church that embraced her with loving hearts. They told her about Jesus and how she could have a fresh start in Him. She gratefully entered the waters of baptism.

Of course, there were many things Liza didn't yet understand in the Word, but she humbly listened, thoughtfully considered, and then tried to practice what she learned. She even began reaching out to others and sharing what Jesus had done for her. Gradually, the sad, devastated woman was transformed by the power of Christ.

The key element in this change was her willingness to receive God's Word along with the counsel of mature believers. Liza's openness and humility helped her find the path of life.

Father, please keep my heart soft and pliable. When things aren't going well, help me listen to the godly counsel of others. In Jesus' name, amen.

True Relationship with God

You have looked into my heart, Lord, and you know all about me (Psalm 139:1, *Contemporary English Version*).

Scripture: **Psalm 139:1-6**
Song: **"God Made Me for Himself"**

Children believe that their parents have the uncanny ability to love them and to know every move they make. For instance, Melissa believes, "My parents have eyes in the backs of their heads." Jeff thinks, "No matter what I do, my mom can always tell when I'm lying." And Abbey says, "Mom and Dad love me, no matter what."

The psalmist expressed some of the same thoughts about his relationship with God. David knew he served an all-seeing, all-knowing, and loving God. He believed that his relationship with God was real because God knew his unspoken thoughts, understood his anger, his anxiety, even his depression.

To have a deepening relationship with God, we must believe that He understands us and His love for us is unconditional. A child put it this way, "When you pray, you get a happy feeling inside—like God just walked into your heart and is warming Himself at a cozy fire."

Lord, You know all about me, yet You invite me to come before You, freely revealing the contents of my heart. What a privilege it is to build my life around You, the one who loves me unconditionally. I thank You in the name of Jesus, my Savior and Lord. Amen.

February 18–24. **Wesley Sharpe** is a retired school psychologist who writes on educational and parenting topics. He lives in Fort Bragg, California.

Test of a Disciple

You cannot be my disciple, unless you love me more than you love your father and mother, your wife and children, and your brothers and sisters. You cannot come with me unless you love me more than you love your own life (Luke 14:26, *Contemporary English Version*).

Scripture: **Luke 14:25-27**
Song: "Jesus Loves Me"

To love Jesus more than life must have seemed unreasonably harsh to many hearers who thought they were Jesus' disciples. And it is not easy for us to hear either. Dr. Phil McGraw, author of *Family First: Your Step-by-Step Plan for Creating a Phenomenal Family,* said, "I love my family more than anything in this world, and I want us all to be safe, healthy, happy, and prosperous in everything we do, both within our family and as we go out into the world."

It is only natural that most of us want to be good parents, and we love those closest to our hearts. Jesus knew that to ask His disciples to put their love for Him above even their closest human relationships meant they were willing to give up everything to serve Him.

Only God can claim this kind of love. Yet, thankfully, when we give Him our all, He gives us every good thing in return: "No mind has conceived what God has prepared for those who love him" (1 Corinthians 2:9).

Gracious God, *I want to build my life around You, to love You more than life itself. Thanks for Your Spirit to help me grow. In Christ's name, amen.*

What Is a Disciple?

So then, you cannot be my disciple unless you give away everything you own (Luke 14:33, *Contemporary English Version*).

Scripture: Luke 14:28-33
Song: "Here I Am, Lord"

Shireen, an Iranian teenager, often listened to the Persian language broadcasts of the Radio Voice of Christ. She wrote the following letter to the station, telling of her wish to follow Jesus:

"One night I saw in a dream that Jesus was telling me, 'My child, I accept you.' I shared these dreams with one of my teachers and one of my friends. They told me if I believed in Jesus I would become an infidel. But when I realized the truth, deep in my heart, I became glad and believed."

She ended her letter with several questions and a request for a Bible and other Christian literature. "Am I a complete Christian now?" She asked. "Is it really true that I am an infidel? And when should I talk to my parents about this?"

Shireen willingly gave up everything to follow Jesus. There must be other stories like hers, because in the past 40 years the Iranian Christian Church has grown from about 5,000 to over 200,000 believers. Her commitment is the kind that Jesus asks from all His followers.

Father, more than anything, I want to be Jesus' disciple. I know that He is always with me, asking me for room in my heart. In His name, amen.

Too Much Money

You still lack one thing. Sell everything you have and give to the poor, and you will have treasure in heaven. Then come, follow me (Luke 18:22).

Scripture: **Luke 18:18-25**
Song: **"Leaving It All with Jesus"**

Marzi Muhammadi, an Afghan doctor, hoped to be elected to the parliament in that country's first free election in 30 years. She was battling for a seat from her province, and to finance her campaign she sold everything she owned except her wedding ring. Yet she lost the election. Still, she willingly gave up everything for her goal.

Marzi's commitment was the kind of response Jesus had hoped for from the man in today's Scripture. But he believed his life was blameless because he followed God's Old Testament law.

Jesus knew that the true test of discipleship for this man would be to give away everything he owned and then follow Him. It was a test of character that the rich man failed. He couldn't bring himself to follow Jesus from place to place or give up his wealth to help others.

Jesus continues to say, "Follow me." If we accept His love and follow His example, we are His disciples. But we will not be perfect in our attempts. Only step by step, relying wholly on His grace, do we stay close to Him.

Lord, *I hand over the control of my life to You, and I will follow Your Spirit's leading the best I can. Thank You for the free gift of salvation that made this journey with You possible. In Jesus' name, amen.*

High Cost of Believing

Peter said, "Remember, we left everything to be your followers!" (Luke 18:28, *Contemporary English Version*).

Scripture: **Luke 18:28-30**
Song: **"Leave It There"**

Christians in Vietnam know what it means to give up everything for their faith. Often local authorities try to persuade believers to give up their belief in Jesus. Their tactics include refusing to give monthly support money to poor Christian families. Thus some Christians give in to the pressure and abandon their beliefs; others stand firm.

Peter and the other disciples watched as Jesus spoke to the rich man. The man seemed to have his heart set on the promise of eternal life, but he wasn't willing to make the sacrifice Jesus required of His followers. Disappointed, he walked away.

Later, Peter reminded Jesus that he and the other fishermen had left their homes and families to be with Him. Peter must have realized that what they had given up for Christ would, in a sense, be repaid with eternal life.

To stay or walk away from Jesus is still the choice we face. Each of us must decide whether the benefits of committing our lives to God are worth the hardships we may have to endure. Thankfully, we need never go it alone. We have the fellowship of other believers to encourage us—along with God's own Spirit within us.

Dear God, *I come to You in obedience to Your Word, trusting in Your gracious promise to be present with me always. In Christ's name, amen.*

A Better Way to Fish

The men pulled their boats up on the shore. Then they left everything and went with Jesus (Luke 5:11, *Contemporary English Version*).

Scripture: **Luke 5:1-11**
Song: **"Follow Me, the Master Said"**

What a difference between the response of the three fishermen who had been washing their nets, and the rich man who asked Jesus the way to eternal life! While the rich man apparently couldn't imagine giving away his wealth, Peter, James, and John didn't hesitate. They left their boats, their nets, and all their other equipment by the lake to follow Jesus.

Can you imagine the disciples saying, "Wait a minute, Jesus! After we sell our fish for a good price, *then* we'll come with You." No, the men had listened to Jesus' teaching, they had witnessed a miracle, and Jesus promised they would do much more than catch fish in the days ahead. They were convinced that Jesus was God's messenger, and they were willing to drop everything to follow Him.

When Jesus turns to us and says "Come with me," there's no room for a wishy-washy response. He seeks a yes or no. And once we say "Yes!" He gives us everything we need to live a life that brings glory to His kingdom.

O God, how I long to be counted among those faithful to Your Son in this life! Keep me close through study of the Word, prayer, and fellowship with my brothers and sisters in the church. Thank You, in Jesus' name. Amen.

Results of Obedience

**The Lord said to Ananias, "Go! I have chosen him to tell for-
eigners, kings, and the people of Israel about me"** (Acts 9:15,
Contemporary English Version).

Scripture: **Acts 9:1-6, 11-16**
Song: **"Trusting Jesus"**

While traveling in the Middle East, we decided to take
a side trip to Damascus, Syria, probably the oldest continually occupied city in the world. We found the ruins of
the ancient Roman city, and after shopping in a crowded
bazaar, we walked the bustling Straight Street mentioned
in Acts 9:11. Later, we walked down a stairway to an
ancient Roman road and entered a small underground
chapel. Tradition says we were standing in the home of
Ananias.

We don't know much about Ananias or how he became
a Christian. But we do know that he swallowed his fear
and immediately obeyed God. He left his home and found
Saul. As a result of his obedience Saul of Tarsus became
Paul the apostle, and the Christian faith spread throughout the Roman world.

Isn't that how God usually works? It may not be clear
to us why He wants us to do something. Nevertheless,
our task is to trust Him and to do what He has called us
to do. He alone is responsible for the results.

*Precious Father, forgive me when I ignore You and go my own way. Give
me the wisdom to recognize Your will and to do it with a joyful heart. Help
me to trust You completely, each step of the way. In Jesus' name, amen.*

This Is Shouting News!

Let everything that has breath praise the LORD. Praise the LORD (Psalm 150:6).

Scripture: **Psalm 150**
Song: **"Praise the Name of Jesus"**

The book of Psalms comes to us in five sections, each division concluding on a note of praise. In fact, this final psalm not only punctuates the fifth section with praise, but also the entire collection of 150 psalms. Yes, the last psalm has the last word, the word of praise. Yet there is one requirement: We have to be breathing. And if we are breathing, we ought to be praising.

This is very practical. If we get up in the morning, read the newspaper, and can't find our name in the obituary column, we ought to start the day on a crescendo of praise! The book of Psalms begins by inviting us to the law as a way of life and ends by inviting us to praise as the use of our very breath.

Have you considered that there is no better use of your breath than to articulate praises to the God of your blessings? In other words, the many ways God blesses us each day is "shouting news"!

Dear God, *I raise my praise for the many and varied ways You bring good things to my life, each and every day. You are gracious and generous, and I am grateful. I praise You now and always; as long as I have breath, I will praise You. In the name of Jesus I pray. Amen.*

February 25–29. **Phillip H. Barnhart** has written 14 books and contributed articles to dozens of publications. Retired, he lives with his wife, Sharron, in Florida.

First, Get Ready

Then David said, "No one may carry the ark of God but the Levites, for the LORD has chosen them to carry the ark of God and to minister before Him forever (1 Chronicles 15:2, *New King James Version*).

Scripture: **1 Chronicles 15:1-3, 11-15**
Song: **"Prepare the Way, O Zion!"**

A minister was having difficulty preparing a particular sermon. Finally, he gave up. "Maybe the Holy Spirit will give me something to say," he said to himself. Standing before the congregation on Sunday morning, God did indeed tell him what to say: "Tell the people you are unprepared."

The first time David tried to move the ark to Jerusalem, he made a mess of things. *That will not happen this time,* David vows to himself and promises the people. Every possible preparation will be made, every detail attended to. David will go by the book this time.

Whatever we do for God warrants good preparation. It shouldn't be left to chance or planned haphazardly. After all, God deserves our best. We should do our homework thoroughly, thread our needles carefully, put the stones precisely in place. When we serve God, we are on a high level and in a large place; there, what we do calls for the best we have and the most we are. And before everything else, getting ready is the key to serving God.

Lord, I want to prepare for what You call me to do. Help me ready my mind and my heart through the gifts You give me. In Jesus' name, amen.

A Hallelujah Heart

David told the leaders of the Levites to appoint their brothers as singers to sing joyful songs, accompanied by musical instruments: lyres, harps and cymbals (1 Chronicles 15:16).

Scripture: **1 Chronicles 15:16-24**
Song: **"The Hallelujah Side"**

David's preparation for getting the ark to Jerusalem included a context for joyful praise. The ark, representing God's covenant with His people, would be lifted to highest glory with shouts of victory and songs of adoration. In each soul would be an amen attitude; in each person gathered, a hallelujah heart.

This dimension of uninhibited joy comes through in the 3-year-old who went to church for the first time. After she and her parents had taken their seats, the lights in the sanctuary were dimmed, and the choir came down the center aisle carrying lighted candles. All was quiet until the 3-year-old started singing in a loud voice, "Happy birthday to you. Happy birthday to you!" Her joy wouldn't stay inside. What was in her heart flowed out everywhere.

Someone asked Joseph Haydn, the composer, why his music was so cheerful. He replied, "I cannot make it otherwise. When I think upon God, my heart is so full of joy, the notes dance and leap from my pen!"

Dear Heavenly Father, *there's a joy deep in my heart about who You are to me. May I put it on my face in smiles and laughter. May I put in on my lips in tributes and praises. All praise to You, in Christ's name. Amen.*

God Strengthens Us

God gave the Levites the strength they needed to carry the chest, and so they sacrificed seven bulls and seven rams (1 Chronicles 15:26, *Contemporary English Version*).

Scripture: **1 Chronicles 15:25-29**
Song: **"O God, Our Help in Ages Past"**

A helpful admonition made its way some time ago into books, onto posters, and taped to refrigerator doors. It spoke of God's help in our lives, promising strength and courage: "There is nothing you and God cannot accomplish together today." It's true, isn't it, that such a combination always makes a majority?

David's first attempt to get the ark to Jerusalem failed. The second one did not. The people prepared, and help came from God. It was God who gave them strength to carry the ark to Jerusalem and get it there safely. It was God who guided each step and empowered every move.

When we look at a mountain we need to climb and fear we can't get to the top, God promises to be with us all the way. When we see a road we need to walk, one that stretches long before us and we wonder if we will ever get to its end, God promises to guide our steps and guard our feet. When we put our hands to a formidable and difficult task, we know we are not alone.

Dear God, *thank You for being with me in all things and in all places. As I begin each undertaking, I feel Your hand on mine. I am invited by Your presence, I am encouraged by Your promise, I am strengthened by Your power. In the precious name of Jesus I pray. Amen.*

Blessings All Around

When David had finished offering the burnt offering and peace offerings, he blessed the people in the name of the Lord (1 Chronicles 16:2, *New American Standard Bible*).

Scripture: **1 Chronicles 16:1-6**
Song: **"There Shall Be Showers of Blessing"**

The day the ark arrived in Jerusalem was a great day in the life of God's people. On that day past failure was forgotten and present accomplishment celebrated. All the preparation had paid off, the objective had been reached. What a day of great blessing!

A man attended a Bible study where the teacher talked of the land promised to Abraham. Thinking about that, the man said, "I already live in the promised land." He didn't have to go anywhere to claim God's promises or gain God's favor. In his daily life he already inhabited the perfect place to enjoy God's goodness. For him, there were blessings all around.

Later on in the Bible study, the discussion focused on the stress people experience these days. This same man commented, "I'm too blessed to be stressed." In a similar vein, an old Russian proverb says, "All days are beautiful . . . when you can wake up." God gives us life, and life gives us so much, if we'll only see it.

Dear Lord, *how extravagant You are in Your blessings! With You, the calf is always the fatted calf, the robe the best robe, the pearl a gem of great price. Your peace, too, exceeds my understanding. Every blessing You give me, I give You back in praise. In Jesus' name I pray. Amen.*

My Prayer Notes

_____

_____

_____

_____

_____

_____

_____

_____

_____

_____

_____

_____

_____

_____

_____

_____

_____

_____

_____

_____

_____

My Prayer Notes